WHOLISTIC FACIAL CARE

BEAUTY THROUGH HEALTH

To Sara,

In Health & Happiness

Leah [illegible]

1999

WHOLISTIC FACIAL CARE

BEAUTY THROUGH HEALTH

by

Leah Dumbrava

Edited by sibylle preuschat

Natural Healing Service, Toronto, Canada

All inquiries should be addressed to:
Natural Healing Service
2350 Dundas St. W. #1706 - A
Toronto, Ontario
Canada, M6P 4B1
Fax: (416)588-5758

Library of Congress Cataloguing in Publication Data
Wholistic Facial Care: Beauty through Health
ISBN 0-9696860-0-5

Cataloguing in Publication Data (CIP) RL87.D85 1993 646.7'26 C93-093728-7

Edited by sibylle preuschat
Illustrations by Dianne Scott

Wholistic Facial Care is available at special discounts for sales, promotions, fund-raising, educational use and premiums. The book is also available at your local health food store and from major book stores in Canada, in the United States and in many countries abroad.

For details contact
The Natural Healing Service
2350 Dundas St. W., #1706-A
Toronto, Ontario
Canada, M6P 4B1
Fax: (416)588-5758

The information in this book is meant to enrich your general knowledge of natural healing, and is not to be taken as professional advice for your specific health problems. Any decision you make involving the treatment of an illness should include the advice of a medical doctor.

Published by the Natural Healing Service, Toronto, Canada,1993

Contents

I dedicate this book to the progress of the wholistic approach to medicine.

I first discovered the concept of wholistic medicine through the work of Bill Baham, Doctor of Chiropractic (D.C.).Through working with hundreds of clients in his chiropractic practice, Dr. Baham realized that to be healed of their ailments, people need not only physical assistance, but emotional, mental and spiritual assistance as well, whatever the whole of their situation requires. As a result, Dr. Baham founded the Whole Health Institute, based in Loveland, Colorado. While still alive, he spoke and taught worldwide on his philosophy of healing. The beautiful spirit of his work continues to inspire many healers as well as people from all walks of life who desire to take more personal responsibility for their own growth.

Introduction

In our society healing is based on treating symptoms and avoiding fundamental problems. Today we are moving closer to mass acceptance of the process of natural healing in most areas. I wrote *Wholistic Facial Care* because I felt such a book was needed to explain a progressive, alternative approach to skin care.

The skin has the power to rejuvenate and repair itself, as it constantly builds new cells. Anyone who wants to get and keep supple, glowing and youthful skin will find this book invaluable. The information presented here will show you how to achieve beautiful skin without using any methods harmful to your physical, emotional or mental well-being.

Underlying the information in this book are fifteen years of work, experience and observation of human nature as well as the wisdom of Japanese and Chinese medicine and Jewish kabbalistic philosophy, preserved over thousands of years.

My own experience of both classical treatment and newly developed beauty methods encouraged me to work with these ancient healing principles to develop a new method of attaining beautiful skin. Wholistic Facial Care is the result. This program uses natural, specially formulated active lotions and essential oils to cleanse and feed the skin, thereby repairing and rejuvenating blemished and problem skin. I have named the products I have invented *Leahder*. *Leahder* is capable of rebalancing any skin type. The external treatment is complemented by food therapy and exercise, to cleanse and strengthen the inner functions which directly influence the appearance of the skin. Wholistic Facial Care offers a natural approach that clears up most skin problems.

Each treatment with *Leahder* leaves your skin soft as silk and glowing with vitality, and your whole body deeply relaxed and refreshed. In addition the Wholistic Facial Care program offers positive steps to delay the aging process. Enhancing the treatments with dietary and lifestyle adjustments will ensure that your skin difficulties never return.

In this book I share the techniques and strategies that I use in my Wholistic Facial Care practise to help my clients look their best.

If you apply the information in this book in a committed way, you will notice a change in skin texture after three to four months. You will no longer need to use creams if you don't wish to and not only your skin but your whole being will be more balanced and healthy, more beautiful.

Part One

Chapter One

Wholistic Facial Care

I have written this book because I wish to express and share my experience in the field of skin care with others. I have seen remarkable results from my Wholistic Facial Care program over and over again. (You will find testimonials from my clients in Chapter Eight.) The program aims to help you achieve beauty through the establishment of strong health. When we are healthy, we live life with enthusiasm, commitment and serenity. Our eyes sparkle. We maintain our natural weight and the beauty of our natural proportions. Our skin feels naturally soft and smooth and keeps its youthful appearance. When you have finished reading *Wholistic Facial Care*, you should have all the information you need to begin a successful personalized beauty oriented health program.

The Genesis of Wholistic Facial Care

This book is the fruit of personal experience. I have always been fascinated with the wonders of the body in which we live, and equally fascinated by natural healing. It is probably little wonder then that I eventually developed Wholistic Facial Care, since I was forced to confront skin problems of my own at an early age.

I developed severe acne while still a girl. My mother took me to see cosmeticians and estheticians for the best treatment available at the time: my face was heated with steam, then the blackheads and pimples were squeezed and extracted. These treatments were very painful, and my skin would remain congested for four to five days afterward. I was embarrassed to let people see my face after a treatment, and this added stress and depression to my mental and emotional state.

At times my skin became infected from the extractions as well.

In addition to these treatment sessions, I used all manner of creams to try to heal my open pores. Nothing worked, and the blackheads that continually, stubbornly reappeared would send me back to an esthetican for more steaming and squeezing. As I grew older, my acne diminished, but the blackheads persisted.

The turning point in my struggle with my skin difficulties occured thirteen years ago, when I developed a fleshy growth beside my right eye. Clearly the treatments and creams were not working, but simply removing my symptoms from sight for brief periods of time. The actual health of my skin was worsening.

I began to research methods of treatment in response to

my own urgent need. This research led me to develop a formula, made of natural ingredients, which I named *Leahder.* Through using *Leahder* on myself, the growth beside my eye gradually disappeared and has not returned. In addition, my blackheads and pimples disappeared and my complexion became clear and healthy.

I developed *Leahder* intuitively, in response to an immediate problem. After my success with it, I desired a more intellectual understanding of why the formula worked. I began a formal study of the natural healing arts, which lasted several years and took me on extensive travels. I learned how the human system functions, how the major organ systems interact, and what conditions support or undermine their optimum functioning. The most important result of my studies was my growing understanding of how the skin interacts with the human system as a whole.

My formal education gave me the confidence I needed to begin treating others. It also supported a growing desire in my life: to create a consolidated program of natural therapies to touch and heal the whole person, with a special focus on the skin. The skin accurately mirrors the relationship between the inner and outer environments. Concentrating on restoring the skin would give me a key to restoring overall health. Furthermore, the appearance and texture of the skin would provide ongoing evidence of how successfully the treatment program is proceeding. The skin itself would guide me to the right methods for each client.

As I slowly began to apply these principles in my work with others, each success and achievement gave me both more intellectual knowledge and greater access to my intuitive healing abilities.

Eventually I felt ready to give my program a name: Wholistic Facial Care. My ongoing work with my clients ensures that Wholistic Facial Care will continue to develop, but the basic structure is now in place firmly enough to make this book possible.

Wholistic Facial Care

Many of us dedicate a great deal of time to looking after the skin on our face, neck and around our eyes as though it were separate from the rest of the self. Only by taking care of our whole selves, physically, emotionally, mentally and spiritually, can we achieve the results we desire.

The Wholistic Facial Care program can rebalance any skin type, whether oily, dry, dehydrated, sensitive, comedone, asphyxiated or combination. Because it is a wholistic approach, it treats both the symptoms and the cause of the problem. I use *Leahder* externally to repair damaged skin. The *Leahder* cosmetic kit contains a formula which removes the dead cells on the surface of the skin, and another which gives the living cells the nutrition they need to function at their best. Regular use of the *Leahder* product creates biological changes in skin texture. At the same time I rebalance the internal system by using or proposing food therapy, exercise, massage and relaxation and breathing exercises in my work with my clients.

If you decide to try my techniques yourself, please

remember that natural healing is not an instant process. It may take some time and a fair amount of effort to bring your whole body, mind and spirit into balance. However, a slow, gentle approach to this task is always worthwhile, for once you have achieved the desired results you know how it was done. Your newfound knowledge will give you the resources you need to sustain your achievement and to prevent any new negative health surprises.

Indeed, one of the big attractions of this type of approach to achieving beautiful skin is the improvement it brings to your general health. Because Wholistic Facial Care treats the whole person, and eradicates the cause of a problem as well as the symptoms, it tones the entire system. Many minor ailments not connected with your skin problems often disappear. Your overall energy and vitality will increase, and life will become more pleasurable.

Anatomy of the Concept

Before you go on to explore and apply the information in this book, I would like to discuss in more abstract terms how Wholistic Facial Care came to be, because I believe your own success with this program depends on understanding a certain type of thinking process.

"Necessity is the mother of invention." A challenge, the necessity of meeting a need, stimulates the creation of new concepts and new techniques. The challenge that faced me after I developed acne was how to return my skin to its natural beauty without having to suffer painful and congesting esthetic treatments.

This challenge set the creative process in motion. In order to emerge with a solution to the challenge, I also had to observe the situation carefully and in depth. By using my powers of creativity and observation in combination I invented *Leahder* and Wholistic Facial Care. Then, by exploring and applying these discoveries, I have been able to continue improving on the original solution to the present day.

If you wish to deal successfully with the challenges facing you, whatever they may be, this same process will help you. Wholistic Facial Care is one option among many. The nature of the challenges facing you will determine the solution you create, using whatever combination of concepts and techniques work for you. Your own personal and practical experience is always your best guide as to what the best solutions are for you.

Now we are ready to explore why it is that we can so effectively create health and beauty in our lives through the use of wholistic principles.

Chapter Two

Why the Skin Reflects the Health of Our Whole Being

In the first chapter I explained that Wholistic Facial Care works as effectively as it does because the program treats the whole person, not just the skin. But why does this matter so much? How does our skin reflect both our inner reality and the environment around us? Once you understand the answers to these questions, you will have the power to use the information in the rest of this book in the way that is most appropriate for you.

We can begin to answer these questions by considering an obvious fact that we probably don't think about most of the time. That is, our skin is part of the whole universe. This fact is simple and obvious, but it has far-reaching implications. I believe there are things we can say about the universe as a whole, that are always true. If these statements apply to everything in the universe, then they apply to our skin as well. I believe the following are such statements:

1)*The entire universe is one unified flow of energy, which knows how it wants to be and what it wants to become. Human choices are part of the being and becoming process of the universe.*

2) Everything is connected to everything else.

3) Everything is in a state of permanent transformation.

Let's consider these statements in more depth.

1) The entire universe is one unified flow of energy, which knows how it wants to be and what it wants to become. Human choices are part of the being and becoming process of the universe.

This idea is so centrally important that it has a chapter all its own, the next one in this book.

2)Everything is connected to everything else.

If you remember that everything is part of one energy, masquerading, playing in an infinity of costumes, this idea is easy to understand in an abstract way. If you want to understand it in a more concrete way, try the following game.

Choose something around you. It can be anything at all. Now choose another thing with which the first thing is connected. The connection can be of any nature. The possibilities are endless. Both the "things" and the "connections" are forms of energy. Now think of a third thing which is connected to the second. Try continuing for at least ten steps, and write down your list as you go. Did you realize before you started that the first and tenth objects on your list were related? That the first and ninth connecting energies had anything to do with one another?

We can only be stopped in this process when we reach the mysterious, the unknown source, what some people call God.

This connecting game can be fun and easy to play, but it is also a powerful way to think. New discoveries and creative solutions to old problems arise when we are willing to look again at the larger picture. The word "heal" means to "make whole." By searching out the connections between one thing and another, which on the surface often appear not to be related at all, we gain the power to heal, because we understand the wholeness of the situation.

3) Everything is in a state of permanent transformation.

Nothing is ever completely identical to anything else, no event can ever be exactly repeated. Even if two things or events are identical in every other way, they will be separated by space or time. No two events or objects can ever be completely identical, of course. Ever shifting dances of attraction and repulsion, giving and receiving constantly alter the world. What we call death is simply part of the never ending universal process of transformation. Through death energy from one form spreads itself into many other forms. We think of death as an ending, but it always begins many things as well.

The quality of each transformation in the world is greatly affected by the other energies that interact with it. We can see this easily when we consider transformations that are common to many people. For example, most people change from children to adults. How easily this change takes place, and what the results are, depends on a person's genetic make-up, culture, character, family life, diet, natural surroundings and a host of other influences.

The concepts I have just outlined above provide a powerful guide to understanding how Wholistic Facial Care works. If our skin is part of the universal energy, connected in endless ways to everything else in the universe, both inside and outside us, then it follows that there will be ways to change the skin's appearance without actually working on the skin itself. I have investigated this possibility in depth. Much of this book shares the results of my research.

Again, with respect to the concepts I have outlined, we can also see that since everything is always transforming itself, our skin too must be always transforming. And this is indeed the case. New cells are constantly being born within our skin. They make their way to the surface where they form the outermost layer of physical protection for our bodies before they die and eventually flake off. *Because of our human ability to manipulate energy according to our values and wishes, we can powerfully influence the direction this ongoing transformative process takes.* We do this by changing the types and qualities of energies that connect with our skin.

To understand this in a less abstract way, consider a simple example from nature. The same kind of tree will have different bark (rougher or smoother, thicker or thinner, darker or lighter in colour) depending on where it grows. How much water does it get? Is the soil rocky or rich? And if the bark is damaged in some way, the healing of the area will result in different bark formations, depending on its original state of health and on how the damaged area is cared for, or not cared for. Our skin responds to its environment in the same way. We, however have much more control over the influences that touch our skin than the tree has.

In my experience, the quality of food energy we take in and how well we digest it, the mental and emotional patterns we habitually allow to fill our consciousness, the outer environment, the air, water, soil and climate that surround us, all exert tremendous influence on our skin.

I will touch on some of these influences now in a more specific way. I will examine in broad outline what energies our skin needs to absorb to become smooth, soft, vital and strong.

Food and Digestion

What we eat and how well we digest it have a major influence on the appearance of our skin. If we don't digest our food efficiently and completely, toxins accumulate in our bodies. These toxins can be incompletely broken down food molecules which interact with our bodies in undesirable ways. Also, if our digestion is weak, or we eat foods difficult to digest, food will stay inside our bodies for too long and begin to ferment and/or coat the inside of our digestive system. This further damages our ability to absorb the nutrition we need. Our bodies attempt to eliminate toxins in any way possible. Thus, poisons produced by ineffective digestion show up as pimples, acne, rough or dry skin, or sagging or puffy skin. In fact, in my experience, almost every skin problem represents our way of telling ourselves that something is wrong with our digestion. Because our skin is on the outside, where we can see it and feel it, our body, in its wisdom, uses it to alert us to inner problems that are harder to detect. Other symptoms such as minor fever, nausea and headaches often function in the same way.

If the digestion functions well, but a skin problem persists, then the eliminative process in the kidneys and lungs is probably not working well, due to damage done by one's lifestyle or environment.

Poor diet, a lifestyle unsuited to the individual, and excessive stress all contribute to digestive disorders. Symptoms of poor digestion include bloating, a burning sensation after meals, an oppressive sense of fullness after eating, constipation and nausea after taking supplements. Later on in this book I will discuss in detail how to strengthen the digestion.

Thoughts and Emotions

You have probably already noticed that worries, anger, fear and an unrelaxed mental state negatively affect your digestion. When you are happy and enjoying life, digestion flows along smoothly as well. Because of the intimate relationship between digestion and the skin, your *habitual* emotional and mental states will affect your appearance for better or worse.

Our habitual thoughts and feelings also affect our appearance through other channels. Thoughts directly affect our central nervous system functioning. If the central nervous system does not function smoothly, this creates biochemical disruptions in our bodies. Over time, the stress on our system will create symptoms, including skin damage.

Again, it is possible to understand this concept in a less abstract way, by trying an experiment. Sit down and let yourself slump in your chair. Create the worst posture possible. Now how do you feel? Where does your mind go? You've probably done this the other way around many times. If you felt depressed or anxious, you slumped or dragged your body, becoming less vital and attractive. The skin, at its own level and in its own ways reflects our thoughts and emotions in the same way our posture does. The happier we are, the better our skin will be, no matter what our age.

Now what happens if we stretch our spine, stand or sit up straight, open our chest and breathe deeply? If something as simple as changing our body posture can shift our mood, we must have a great deal of control over our mental and emotional state. By determining to cultivate mental and emotional balance, we also become more beautiful. I will introduce in greater detail throughout this book techniques that increase emotional and mental health.

The Environment

It is true that the climate in which we live will present challenges to the skin. But we are part of nature and natural remedies can solve problems caused by atmospheric conditions. If we eat the foods that grow in our area in the seasons in which they appear and exercise out of doors frequently we will be in greater harmony with the conditions in which we live. We may also wish to supplement this lifestyle with the use of *Leahder*, to give extra nourishment and protection to the skin.

Far more threatening to our health and our body than the natural climate are the many unbalanced conditions we have as a species created in our environment. Electromagnetic fields disrupt the organized pattern of our individual electric and magnetic energy. Air pollution and water pollution damage the lungs and kidneys, whose crucial job it is to eliminate metabolic wastes from the body. Poisonous pesticides, herbicides, hormones, antibiotics, radioactivity, and fallout from air pollution all contaminate our food supply. The depletion of the ozone layer in the upper part of the earth's atmosphere by various chemicals poses a direct threat to the skin. As the ozone thins, more of the sun's ultra-violet rays reach our skin. These cause premature aging, skin cancer and cataracts in the eyes as well.

Nowadays it is necessary for each one of us to keep our health at the highest level possible so that we can ward off as much as possible the effects of environmental pollution. Chapter 6 contains more detailed information on dealing with pollutants.

Conclusion

To begin this chapter we asked the question, "How does our skin reflect both our inner state and the external environment?" We have now answered that question, both in principle and with respect to specific connections between the skin and the digestion, thoughts, feelings, and outside environment.

To apply this information, you will need to keep it in context - your own context. Remember that "Everything is in a state of permanent transformation." No two skin difficulties are ever completely alike. Even if the same kind of problem is found in the same area of the skin in two people, my treatment for each would be different because the causes of the problem would be different. One person might have a pimple due to the stress of taking an exam; another might experience the same problem after a death in the family. In a third case, poor diet might be causing the outbreak. In each case, the individual's age, diet, lifestyle, personal make-up and surrounding circumstances will also affect the rhythm at which the skin clears. By keeping the whole situation in mind, lasting success becomes possible.

Analysis alone, however, does not provide the needed level of perception. Through a consideration of energy flow and its relationship to health and sickness, the next chapter outlines what we need to know to achieve a consciousness capable of perceiving the whole of a situation.

Chapter Three

Energy

The entire universe is one unified flow of energy, which knows how it wants to be and what it wants to become. Human choices are part of the being and becoming process of the universe.

We human beings have the power to shift, interrupt, slow down, speed up, or coax into new patterns the flow of energy that exists all around us and inside us. Our values directly motivate the choices we make. If we stay in tune with our environment as a whole, our manipulations of energy will dance in harmony with the broader ebbs and flows. If, however, we shut our minds and bodies to the whole picture, we are likely to make unbalanced judgements. We block needed energies or allow unneeded energies to flood us.We experience the resultant imbalance as unhappiness and sickness.

We need to learn how to sense our own pace within the universe, our own pathway of growth and unfolding. We need to work in cooperation with our authenticity in order to be in harmony with the whole of existence.

Dialogue

Dialogue can help us achieve such a state. This powerful tool can help us find truth, to sense the flow of energies around us and within us accurately. Once we can make such discernments, we have the information we need to respond appropriately and create a fulfilling and happy life.

To reach the truth, we must learn to enter into dialogue with ourselves, with the people around us, with our surrounding environment, and with nature. Once we begin a dialogue with these others, ideas take on new dimensions which otherwise remain closed. As others respond to us with their observations and reflections, the dialogues illuminate what is lacking in our own thinking and approach. Through this process we begin to see the wider implications of our beliefs. Dialogue also clarifies misinterpretations due to unclear expression on one side or misunderstanding on another.

Thus dialogue increases our knowledge and understanding and therefore our ability to prevent problems of all kinds, including health problems. Dialogue is a basic necessity for maintaining our health as a *whole.*

The concept of dialogue is extremely useful in the case of symptoms or illness as well. As I mentioned in the previous chapter, most symptoms (skin problems, fever, nausea, headaches, colds, lack of energy, physical disturbances) are a sign that something is not working properly within our bodies, in the environment which affects us, or most likely, both. If we can learn to dialogue with our symptoms, rather than try to stop or suppress them, we will be able to find their real cause. Once we know that, we can address it, rather than fight the symptoms, and so guarantee our continuous health.

Addressing Energy Disturbances

The real cause of our symptoms will always be an energy disturbance of some kind. The flow of energy as it wishes to be when the whole of ourself is taken into account will have been denied in some way. Perhaps we have not rested when we felt tired, or conversely, we held ourselves back from working at something we really wanted to achieve. Perhaps a pollutant has interfered with a body function. Whatever the case, our desired pattern of energy flow has been distorted. The disturbances may be at the physical, emotional, mental or spiritual level, or at two or more of these levels at once.

To begin restoring healthy energetic expression, we need will and faith, working together. If we break the connection between our will and our faith, we will experience failure. Only when the connection is reestablished can a positive process begin to work.

WILL + FAITH = SUCCESS

WILL vs. FAITH = FAILURE

Put another way, when we decide to heal a problem or

improve a situation, we hamper our own progress if we don't have faith in the solution we have chosen. When we believe in the healing technique we have elected, regardless of what it is, it still has the power to cure us. Our faith is strongest if we understand the method we have chosen and why, and we then take full responsibility for our choice.

If we decide to try a wholistic approach, such as Wholistic Facial Care, we also need to keep in mind that such a method requires perseverance. There will be many new skills to learn, and it will take some time before we become fully competent with them. A wholistic approach also works gently and usually at the pace we can handle, even if we consciously desire greater speed. It is especially unreasonable to expect a condition to disappear overnight if it has evolved gradually. A slow healing process is necessary in this case, to avoid shocking the system. Often the slow pace also allows us to dialogue with all our symptoms one by one, bringing mental and emotional healing to accompany the physical changes.

Patience and perseverance are also needed in a wholistic approach because often more problems will come to the surface and ask for our attention once the healing process has started. This happens because as we become stronger, our system becomes strong enough to bring deeper problems to the surface where we can become aware of them.

By calling on your resources of courage, patience, tolerance, strength and understanding, you will be able to make the health program of your choice work for you, especially if you remain flexible as well and continue expanding your knowledge with dialogue. Willingness to make use of a wide range of treatments, including conventional medicine, if it provides the needed solution in a given situation, will increase your chances of success.

Irritability and impatience, on the other hand, weaken mental, emotional and physical stability.

Stress

We become irritable and impatient, of course, when we are stressed. In fact, unrelieved tension can change the normal biochemistry of the body and create serious illness. We feel stress when there is a gap between life as it is and life as we would like it to be.

Two approaches are needed to deal with this gap. If it has been caused by injustice or irresponsibility on ours or somebody else's part, we can turn stress into a motivation for positive action, and work to find creative solutions to the situation. On the other hand, we often create a stressful gap between life as it is and life as it should be by having too many rigid expectations of what should be. The more inflexible we are, the more likely we will get upset when life doesn't conform to our wishes. Life has its own flow and agenda, and our desires are only part of the picture. We can learn to rejoice in its offerings.

If your circumstances seem particularly difficult, you can encourage yourself with the certain knowledge that life is perpetual motion. Never be disheartened. Instead, practise patience and integrity in the midst of your difficulties and you will eventually find yourself pleasantly surprised by the directions life begins to take.

Many skin problem sufferers will confirm that when things are going according to plan, their skin improves. When life is not going their way, their skin becomes worse again. To overcome this tendency, we can learn to live from our centre. Then we will begin to approach a state in which life is always going our way.

Living from the Centre

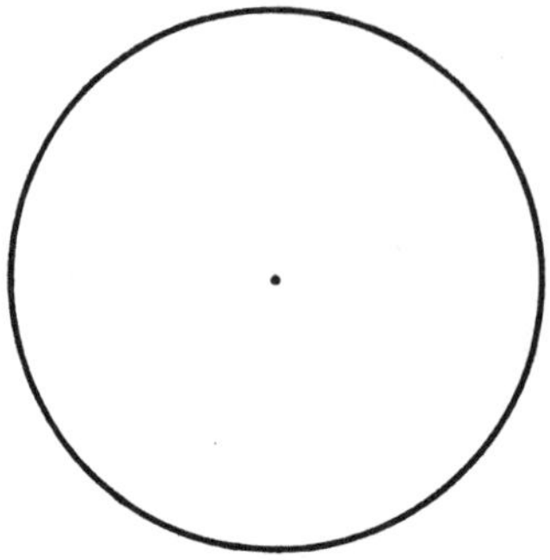

Figure 1.

This ancient symbol expresses the truth that the centre and the circle need each other.

Once you understand the potency of this image, you will desire to know your own centre.

Picture yourself as a miniature solar system. In the centre is your spirit (like the sun) surrounded by your mind and body. When we acknowledge the spirit within us, we gain balance and continuity in our lives. If we do not acknowledge our spirit, we become confused.

Without a centre on which to focus ourselves, we cannot reap the benefits of being aware of our own wholeness.

Many of us nowadays no longer know what our spirit is.

The best way to learn is to experience it for ourselves. Although the word spirit may suggest intangible, untouchable realities, the simplest ways to reach the spirit come through the physical world.

We can start with our body. Sit or lie down comfortably, breathe deeply, and allow your attention to rest on the centre of your chest - your heart chakra. (The chakras will be discussed in more detail in Chapter 4.) Then simply ask your heart to open. Taking a few moments now and then to do this will begin putting you in touch with your spirit.

Another way to get in touch with your spirit is to spend time in natural surroundings, observing what happens in nature. Within a short time, you will begin to feel more secure and less afraid of death. Given the opportunity, the forces of nature always harmonize, rebuild, rebalance and refresh us.

Many of us pursue this healing without consciously realizing it. We can hardly wait to spend vacation time at the seashore or the cottage. There, close to the water, the earth, the wind and the stars, we rediscover our blissful connection to all of existence. Such times present a special opportunity, if we can listen lovingly and respectfully, to hear the voice of our own spirit guiding us. We will become increasingly aware of how it is best for us to eat, drink, act, think and feel in any situation.

When we live in harmony with our own spirit, the cosmic spirit responds. An exchange begins between us and the ultimate power or cosmic intelligence. It is our connection with the ultimate power, however we name it, that makes us completely whole beings.

The growth of our relationship with spirit brings us into deeper and deeper love. We will see totally new dimensions of the world we live in.

Life will continue to present us with stresses and challenges, but when we are in tune with our spiritual centre, our direction becomes stronger and stronger and even difficulties no longer seem so oppressive. Instead we become able to learn and benefit from obstacles, so that they help us to achieve our goals.

Expanding the Circle

The more of us that make the concepts in this chapter a dynamic part of our own lives, the more our whole society will change.

I especially hope to see the healing arts become less fragmented. If the different groups involved in healing, including conventional medical practitioners, could enter into truthful and open dialogue with one another, better health care for all could be achieved.

It is also my dream that someday soon we will construct homes and public buildings with circular rooms, not square ones, as many African and indigenous North American societies do. Circular rooms promote tranquility and the balanced circulation of energy throughout the space, bringing well-being and happiness to the inhabitants.

Part Two

Introduction to Chapters Four, Five, Six and Seven

The first three chapters introduced you to the conceptual framework which supports the birth of wholistic healing methodologies such as Wholistic Facial Care. At this point you are aware that the health and beauty of your skin depends on a balanced energy flow through both your internal and external environments. Symptoms such as pimples, blemishes, blackheads, oily skin, dry skin, tired looking or puffy skin all indicate a disturbance of energy flow somewhere in the system. The next four chapters introduce you to an array of methods that have been developed by wholistically oriented healing practitioners for restoring disturbed energy flow to its balanced state. All these methods support and complement one another.

Chapter 4, *Help Along the Way: Working with Energy*, describes wholistic healing methodologies which can be used as needed to catalyze and support deep, longterm changes.

Chapter 5, *The Importance of Internal Cleansing,* discusses the value of an internal cleansing program to the maintenance of health and the appearance of the skin. I explain how to strengthen the digestive organs, eliminative organs, mind and emotions.

Chapter 6, *A Daily Routine,* explains the elements of a health and beauty supportive daily routine. I offer suggestions on diet, exercise, relaxation, and protection against environmental contaminants.

Chapter 7, *Another Option: Treatment from a Certified Wholistic Facial Care Practitioner,* describes what to expect if you decide to work with a certified Wholistic Facial Care practitioner, and also gives step by step directions for a complete facial with *Leahder.*

If you combine a daily routine which promotes your health and happiness (Chapter 6) with the use of *Leahder* (Chapter 7) and the wholistic healing techniques and internal cleansing programs outlined in Chapters 4 and 5, you are sure to be rewarded with beautiful, smoothly textured skin.

Depending on your own inclinations and needs, you may wish to read these chapters in an order different from the one presented here.

Reading the first section of Chapter 4, "Face/Body Interconnectedness," may help you to decide how to approach these chapters. The crucial importance of proper breathing to the success of any of the methods presented in the next three chapters should also be kept in mind. "Breathing" is the second section of Chapter 4.

Chapter Four

Help Along The Way: Working With Energy

Wholistic healers have been developing and using the techniques described in this chapter for centuries, and in some cases, for millennia. Each technique is safe, with no dangerous side effects, so long as the practitioner is properly qualified and sincerely committed to helping his or her clients.

You can use these techniques to address a specific problem, to catalyze healing energies in general, and for stress management. Your intuition, open dialogue with therapists, and some trial and error will prove your best guides to decide which methods will work most effectively for you at any given time.

Before describing the various healing techniques, I will briefly touch upon the traditional Chinese medical view of the face. This information may help you determine where your own pathway to better health begins.

Face/Body Interconnectedness

In Chapter 2, I explained that everything is interconnected. Traditional Chinese medical practitioners have studied the nature of these interconnections for at least three thousand years. They have found that certain patterns of relatedness repeat themselves. One of these repeated patterns is the way the human body and face relate to each other.

Traditional Chinese medicine calls the head and face the upper sphere of the body, while the torso and limbs are the lower sphere. The upper sphere gives signals to the lower which help it to function properly, and vice versa. One obvious example of the way the upper sphere guides the lower is through the functioning of the senses. What we hear, see, smell and taste inspires action in the body. On the other hand, what we feel and know "in our gut" affects our perception of situations and our verbal and analytical response.

The interplay between the two spheres occurs at more subtle levels as well. Each area of the head and face correlates to organs in the body. The appearance of the facial skin in a particular area relates to how well the corresponding organ is functioning.

The face is divided into three major areas. These correspond to the internal organs as follows:

1) *Around the mouth.* This area relates to the digestive system. Skin problems here indicate that the digestion must be strengthened. The specific organs involved are the stomach, spleen, pancreas, liver, gall bladder, small intestine and large intestine.

2) *Middle area of the face, up to the eye brows.* Pimples, blemishes, discoloured skin (usually under the eyes) and other problems in this area indicate disturbances in the cir-

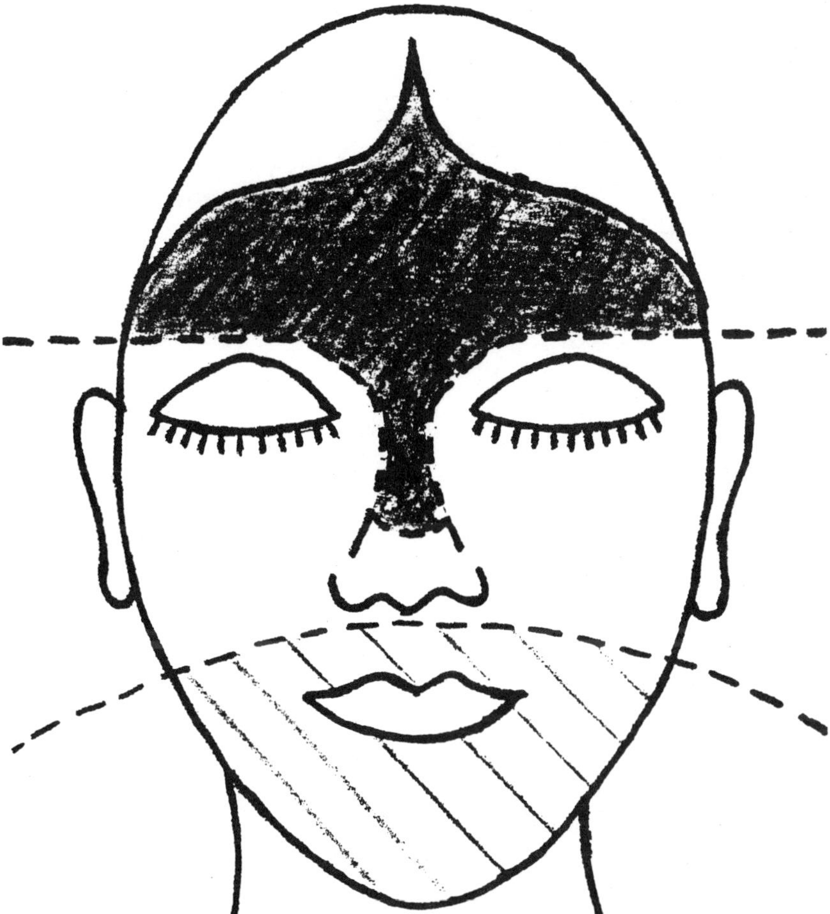

Figure 2. Face/Body Interconnectedness

culatory, respiratory and eliminative systems. The specific organs involved are the heart, lung and kidneys.

3) *The forehead.* The appearance of the forehead reflects the health of the entire nervous system, which includes the spinal cord.

It is because of these interconnections that Wholistic Facial Care works so effectively. The program works to heal the organs, and so immediately influences the appearance of the face. These interconnections also explain why the facial touch sequence described in Chapter 7 harmonizes and relaxes the whole body.

By considering carefully the general pattern of outbreaks or problem areas on your face, you can gain a sense of the internal areas which need to be strengthened.

Breathing

When breathing stops, life ends very quickly. The deeper and fuller our habitual breathing pattern is, the stronger and more vital we will be at every level of our existence. Even if we adhere to the healthiest diet and lifestyle possible, and receive treatments from the most dedicated practitioners, if we do not breathe with commitment and enthusiasm our full potential will not be attained. Breathing well is the foundation of all healing.

For most of us, breathing is unconscious and poorly developed, insufficient for supporting high vitality. Often our inhalations are so weak that we hardly use our diaphragm. Begin breaking this habit by taking an occasional deep breath with a long and deep exhalation. The important thing is to use the diaphragm to the fullest. Whenever possible, breathe this way at least three times in a row, and make sure to practise your deep breathing daily. Over time, your breathings habits as a whole will change.

Deep breathing benefits the skin by toning the eliminative organs. Breathing well also helps ensure that your entire system is well nourished. All the cells need a steady and plentiful supply of oxygen to function at their best. With this nourishment, they will digest your food better, and eliminate metabolic wastes more efficiently.

Deep breathing can also help balance our state of mind and the overall functioning of our central nervous system. When your nerves are feeling frayed or jangled, use deep breathing as a natural tranquilizer that has no harmful side effects. (For specific breathing and relaxation exercises, please see Chapter 6.)

Breathing can also help to detach us from ordinary ego focussed awareness. When stressed, or simply desiring to relax, try breathing on the physical level only, leaving all mental and emotional activity aside for the moment. Nothing else matters; you are breathing. Doing this allows consciousness to relax totally and so improves health. Through this practice we discover that breath is the essence of being.

The basic components of the respiratory system are shown in Figure 3.

The remainder of this chapter will briefly describe the following wholistic therapies: Affirmations, Aromatherapy,

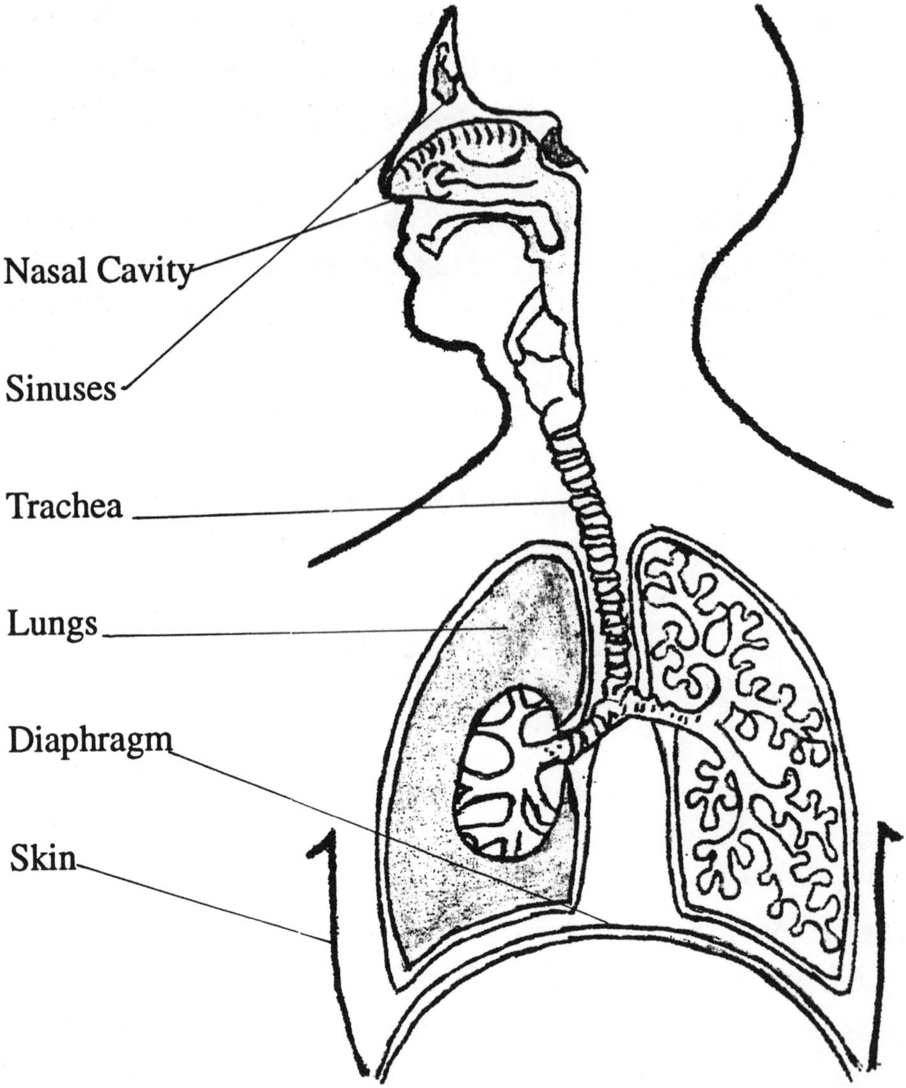

Figure 3. The Respiratory System

Chakra Work, Chiropractic Treatment, Colon Irrigation, Cupping, Homeopathy, Naturopathy, Reflexology, Reiki, Shiatsu and Therapeutic Environments. Use these descriptions as initial clues to what might help restore any health difficulties you have.

For more detailed information about these and other wholistic therapies, consult the excellent books and magazines available in most health food stores, women's bookstores, "New Age" bookstores and public libraries. Most wholistic practitioners are happy to discuss their work with prospective clients. Many also have brochures available which describe the nature of their practice.

Affirmations

Sometimes we need to be encouraged by hearing the right word at the right moment. When this affirmative word does not arrive from another, we can create what we need from our own resources. We are a major source of what we need, if we can only remember that fact.

Affirm to yourself whatever you need: I want; I believe; I see it; I am strong; I am not alone, I am with myself; I am capable; I know what I want; I will do it because I believe it; there is always another option, always an avenue; nothing is the end of the world. Remind yourself that you can always find a new beginning, a new connection, a new direction, or a new solution.

Do not let yourself be limited by barriers, give yourself another chance to solve the problem. And although something seems unattainable today, you just never know what tomorrow will bring. There are always unpredictable leads, unpredictable opportunities, and unpredictable changes.

If a change seems undesirable, try looking at it as an interesting learning opportunity. Change is always a new beginning. Your attitude can ensure that all changes lead to greater health in the end. If you practise forgiveness, love and understanding in every situation, you will be able to discern the direction best for you to take.

One affirmation I use regularly is the simple phrase, "Be positive." By saying it to myself several times in a loud voice and positive attitude, I find it helps to relieve stressful situations.

No matter what affirmations you choose to use to keep your outlook positive and creative, you will be avoiding damage to your health. Affirmations keep your mood calmer and your mind and emotions more relaxed and responsive during the passage through difficult moments.

Aromatherapy

Aromatherapy uses essential oils as therapeutic agents. Essential oils are concentrated liquid extracts, not "oily" in the usual sense, which are distilled from certain plants. They evaporate quickly when placed in contact with heat. They are best distilled at specific times of the year, which are different for each plant.

Essential oils represent the pure spirit of the plant. They carry its vital characteristics, including its scent. The aromatic oils of flowers, leaves, roots and bark work potent magic on the body and mind. Their beneficial properties have been known for centuries.

In kabbalistic sources, which concern Jewish mysticism, oil is a metaphor for the soul of the holy writings. Oil signifies a distilled essence distinct and separate from everything while at the same time pervading everything. Oil is also a metaphor for our own soul. It gives light to the world just as the soul gives light to the body.

Both the Old and New Testaments speak of the uses of oils and water in healing disease. *Leahder,* the foundation of Wholistic Facial Care, is also made of these natural, mysteriously powerful elements.

In my experience, essential oils act on people on many different levels at once. They have strong healing effects on the physical plane. Their fragrances have profound rebalancing effects on the emotions. They comfort, soothe and elevate our spiritual nature.

Aromatherapy can take several different forms:

1) *Massage with essential oils.* The combination of a caring touch with the sensual fragrance of the oils makes massage centred aromatherapy an enjoyable approach to relieving the stresses of everyday life. The oils quickly penetrate, pervade and soothe the entire skin, and also boost blood circulation.

2) *Internal use.* Currently used this way mainly by doctors in Europe, essential oils can be taken internally on their own, or in combination with herbal remedies to heal infections.

3) *Reflexology*. (See the section on reflexology later in this chapter.) After working on the reflex points on a client's feet, reflexologists often use an essential oil to relax all the points and finish the treatment. These practitioners have found that using essential oils on the foot benefits the whole system, since the soles of the feet have a high density of nerve receptors.

To see for yourself how receptive the feet are, try a few drops of one of the relaxing essential oils (lavender, geranium, sandalwood) in a warm foot bath as a way of relieving sleeplessness or headaches.

4) *Bathing*. Try adding essential oils to your baths to relax and strengthen your whole being. I will conclude the section on Aromatherapy with a list of some of the oils and their major properties, to assist you in choosing the oil you need at any given time.

5) *Wholistic Facial Care*. I use essential oils to help my clients reach deep emotional and mental relaxation. I dip a facecloth in a mixture of warm water and an essential oil, and drape this over a client's face.

Smell connects us to parts of our being that no other sense reaches. I believe that the natural smells of these oils reconnect us to nature on a deep level, relaxing us and relieving our stress in a way nothing else can do. Reharmonizing ourselves with nature brings out our natural beauty.

Essential Oils for the Bath

The easiest way to use essential oils at home is in the bath. Following is a list of common oils and their use.

For stress relief : Geranium, Lavender, Sandalwood.

Refreshment/Revitalization: Basil, Bergamot, Peppermint, Rosemary.

Relief of soreness, aches, stress: Eucalyptus, Lavender, Rosemary, Sage.

Relief of arthritis, rheumatism: Eucalyptus, Juniper.

For skin disorders: Black Pepper, Rosemary.

For nervous tension: Lavender.

To soothe emotions, calm anger: Rose.

To relieve coughs, colds: Chamomile, Eucalyptus.

For colds, you may also find chamomile vapour useful. Fill a bowl with very hot water, add a few drops of chamomile essential oil, and breathe in the steam by holding your face over the bowl and draping a towel over both your head and the bowl to trap the steam.

Chakra Work

The chakras are special points in our body that transform universal energy into our own life energy. "Chakra" is a Sanskrit work, which in its meaning describes these points as places where we will the exchange of life force energy between ourselves and the universe. There are estimated to be about 300 chakras in the body.

Each chakra draws in its own special vital energy from

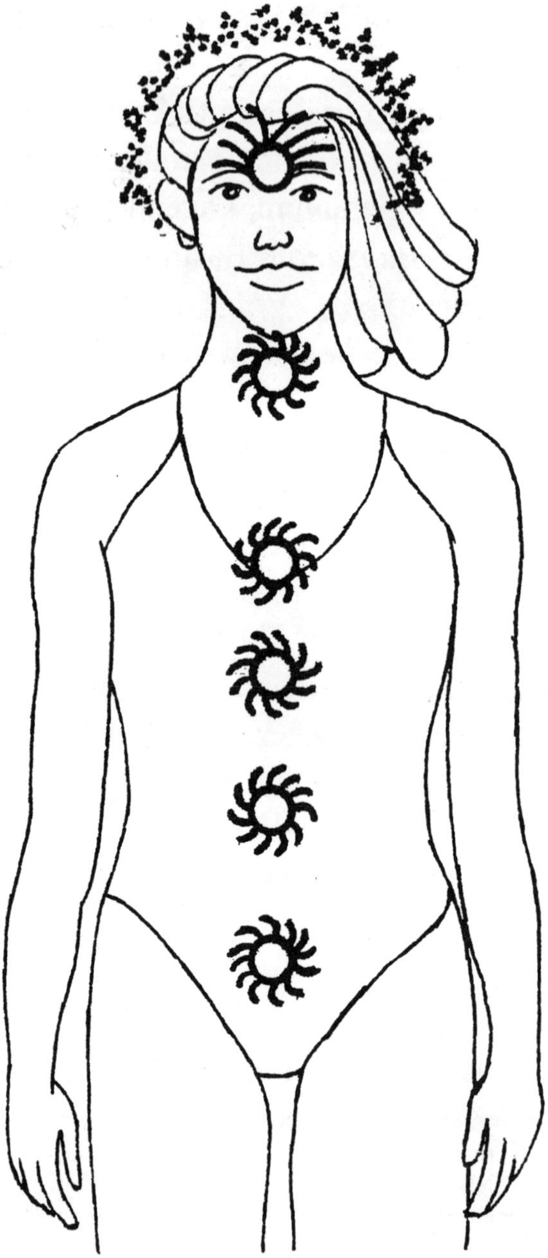

Figure 4. The Chakras

the universe, which is transformed and redistributed throughout our bodies. If you find this difficult to grasp, you can think of eating and digesting food as somewhat similar to chakra activity. We take something different from us in through our mouths, and transform it into ourselves. If the digestion does not work properly, we do not get all the food energy we need. In the same way, if our chakras are blocked or unbalanced we will lack vital energies of some type.

The seven major chakras, as shown in Figure 4, are the best place to start when beginning to work with these energy centres. Each of the chakras described below opens along the back of the body as well, on points opposite the opening in front.

1) The first chakra, located at the base of the spine, connects us to the abundance of the material universe.

2) Two inches below the navel, the second chakra is the seat of our most fundamental emotions.

3) The third chakra is located two to three inches above the navel in the centre of the solar plexus. If this chakra is functioning well, we will usually be able to achieve our own aims at our own pace while remaining a harmonious member of our social group.

4) The heart chakra, the fourth, in the centre of the chest, is associated with our ability to express and accept personal love.

5) The fifth chakra, in the hollow of the throat, regulates our will to communicate.

6) The sixth chakra, our "third eye" is found between the eyes, slightly above the eyebrows. This chakra regulates

intuitive and artistic abilities.

7) The crown chakra on top of the head allows us to communicate with divinity.

In my Wholistic Facial Care practice I use healing touch and music to balance the chakras. Please see the facial touch diagrams in Chapter 7 for an introduction to some of these techniques.

You can also work with your chakras on your own. Try the following.

Lie down comfortably. Place your right hand, fingers closed, on your third chakra, the solar plexus. Place your left hand, fingers also closed, on your sixth chakra, the third eye. After a few minutes you will feel increased warmth and energy.

If you suffer from morning numbness in your hands, hold them, fingers closed, over the second chakra on the belly. You will feel the numbness disappear.

You can experiment with all your chakras in a similar way to find effects helpful to your life.

Placing your hands, with fingers closed, over any painful place in the body will generally ease the discomfort.

Chiropractic Treatment

Chiropractic doctors are highly trained professionals. They relieve bodily pain and stiffness, restore the capability for normal movement to joints and muscles, and help fibrous nodules in the muscle tissue to disappear through specialized, painless manipulations of the body. Because our entire nervous system connects to the spine, chiropractic care of the back also improves the functioning of the organs and perceptual systems. When nerves are relieved of pressures caused by tight muscles and misaligned vertebrae, they become able to carry signals and regulate body functioning more smoothly.

Chiropractic treatment will improve your posture. Once you are using your body properly you are less likely to injure yourself. Greater well-being, self-esteem and confidence usually accompany improved posture as well.

Some chiropractors use acupressure and cupping to complement their work. Acupressure is an ancient Chinese healing technique in which specific points are pressed to relieve stiffness and stress and to create more balanced energy flow in specific areas of the body. Cupping has its own section in this chapter.

Chiropractic care harmonizes well with the Mitzvah Technique. Mitzvah Technique teaches us how to perform everyday movements, such as sitting, standing, walking, in such a way as to avoid a build-up of muscle tension. Accumulated tension from habitually poor movement can lead to back pain, neck pain, sciatica and related conditions.

Colon Irrigation

You may wish to read Chapter 5 for in-depth information on internal cleansing before making a final decision as to whether to receive colonic irrigation.

Since the colon is the major organ of elimination of

digestive wastes, any problem which causes it to malfunction will negatively affect the whole system. Poor diet, stress and lack of exercise can all contribute to poor colon functioning. When deposits of waste matter build up on the walls of the colon, constipation, diarrhea, skin problems or lack of energy may all result.

Colon irrigation can solve these problems. It is a therapy useful for almost anyone, except small children, who do not need it. It is especially indicated in cases of chronic problems with digestion or bowel function. Although many people find the idea of having colon irrigation threatening, frightening or embarrassing, the treatment is painless and the therapists are trained professionals who treat their clients with respect and understanding.

In a colonic treatment the therapist inserts into your rectum a sterile proctoscope which is connected to a tube and water tank. The clean, warm water flows into the colon. By blocking and releasing the exit tube, the therapist will create the conditions needed to allow toxins, mucus and old waste matter to drain out with the water. After a number of colonics, all parts of the colon will be clean. Acidophilus should be taken when having colonic treatment to ensure that intestinal bacteria, necessary for good health, are replaced.

Colon irrigation benefits the skin by removing toxins from the system and lightening the burden on all the eliminative organs. Colonic treatment also improves blood circulation and the functioning of the central nervous sytem.

Cupping

Cupping is a Chinese healing technique over three thousand years old. Today acupuncturists, chiropractors and traditional healers may all practise cupping.

When cupping, the practitioner takes glass cups of different sizes, depending on where they will be placed, and briefly holds burning cotton which has been dipped in alcohol inside the mouth of the cup. Taking care that the edge of the cup is not too hot, the practitioner places them, mouth down, on various parts of the body, as shown in Figure 5. As the air in the cup cools down, a vacuum is created inside the cup. This vacuum sucks out excess moisture and leaked blood. It gives the body a powerful opportunity to release toxic and unwanted material. After ten to fifteen minutes, the practitioner releases the cups by pressing down with them on the skin. This lets more air into the cup and destroys the vacuum.

The treatment leaves pink, red, or sometimes black circles and marks on the skin which disappear within a week.

Cupping effectively removes feelings of dampness and chilliness, loosens stiff joints, and increases resistance to disease. It clears up congested areas in the body and effectively heals bronchitis, asthma, pneumonia, pleurisy, rheumatism, arthritis, migraine and other types of headaches.

Homeopathy

Homeopathy is a highly developed science of healing which nowadays exists in two forms, classical homeopathy

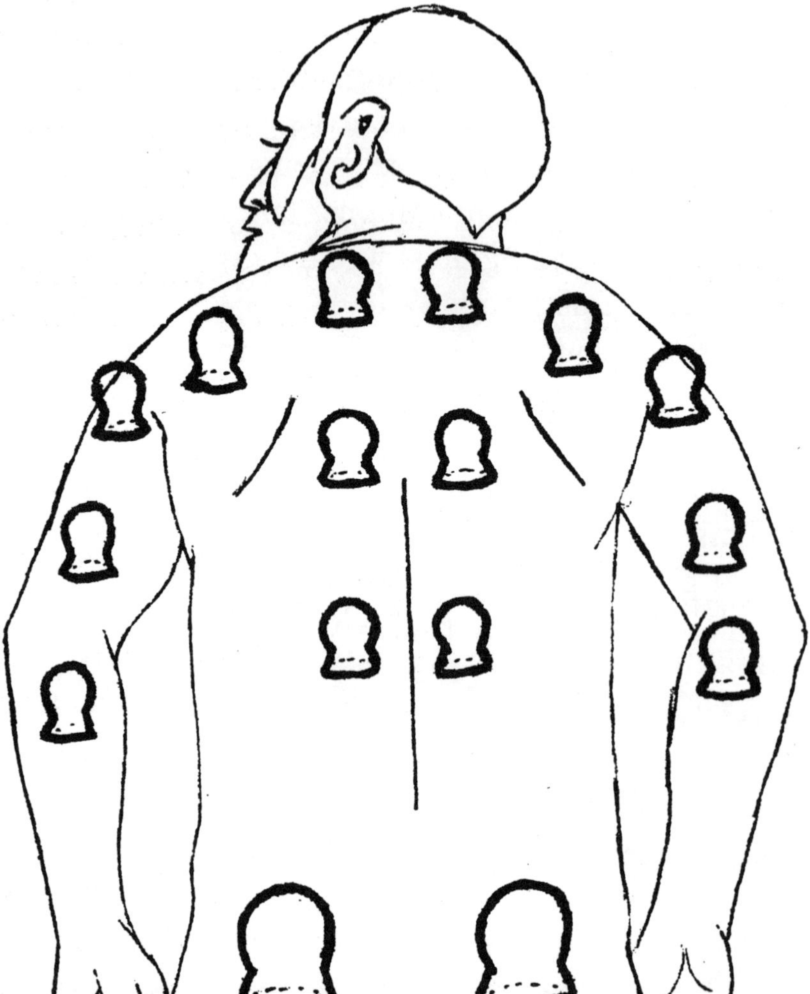

Figure 5. Cupping

and complex homeopathy. Classical homeopathy, often referred to as Hahnemannian homeopathy was founded by Samuel Hahnemann in the eighteenth century.

If you visit a classical homeopath, he or she will interview you at length to create as complete a picture as possible of your health complaints. In a homeopath's eyes, each individual has a unique pattern of illness. This pattern is considered part of a person's whole life process. The practitioner takes into account the effect of outer circumstances, patterns of thinking and feeling, physical symptoms and how they have all interacted with one another in specific sequences during the growth of the illness.

Once a complete picture of the illness has emerged, the homeopath prescribes a remedy. This will be a substance found in nature. If it were to be taken by a healthy person, the substance would create the same, or a very similar, pattern of symptoms as in the illness it is being used to heal. In homeopathy, the sick person receives the substance in extremely diluted form.

Because the substance creates the same symptoms as the illness it is being used to heal, the patient's body gains from it an understanding of what the problem is. It's almost as though the remedy demonstrates the nature of the difficulty by *example*, since it induces the same symptoms as are being experienced. Once the body understands the illness, it becomes able to mobilize its own healing forces effectively to create healthier order and return to well-being once more.

Homeopathic healing usually occurs outside the awareness of everyday consciousness. Sometimes, however, a remedy will bring to conscious awareness buried memories of a trauma that initiated illness in the first place. In this case the homeopath might refer you to a psychotherapist, for help in dealing with the formerly repressed material.

Like all naturally oriented practitioners, a homeopath will encourage you to follow a healthy diet and lifestyle. Otherwise you will expend your vital energy on repairing constantly renewed damage, rather than on healing illness and creating stronger health.

A classical homeopath uses only one remedy at a time. He or she evaluates its effects carefully as the treatment progresses, as a guide to further intervention. A practitioner of complex homeopathy does not pay as detailed attention to the unique individuality of each case. Such a practitioner usually prescribes several of the most common remedies for an illness at once, and bases his or her choices on a more conventional medical model of diagnosis.

Both forms of homeopathy obtain excellent results, and cause no harmful side effects. Again, it is your intuition which will guide you to the healer you need.

Naturopathy

Naturopathic doctors are highly trained professionals. They believe that disease symptoms indicate that our body is working to reject illness by throwing off the poisons which create it. Toxic accumulation in the body may be caused by environmental pollution, lack of sunlight, lack of exercise, lack of rest and relaxation, improper or insufficient nutrition, or other factors stressful to health. They also believe that we have the power to heal ourselves. If we are properly assisted by natural therapies in eliminating toxins and rebuilding healthy functioning, disease will have no chance to take root at deep levels and health will be maintained.

Naturopathic doctors use herbal remedies, vitamin and mineral supplements, massage, physiotherapy, homeopathic remedies, botanical medicines and other non-toxic procedures to assist the body in its healing work.

Reflexology

Reflexology was founded five hundred years ago in India and China, sharing the same roots at origin as acupuncture. Reflexology shares a conceptual framework with facial diagnosis and shiatsu. Like those techniques, it is based on the observation that specific points on the outside of the body reflect the health and functioning of correlated inner organs.

Reflexologists have charted the areas of the feet, called reflexes, corresponding to every part of the body through longitudinal energy channels. The reflexes exist just below the skin. A reflexology practitioner has studied body systems in depth and uses that knowledge to determine the fundamental causes or origins of symptoms.

The practitioner applies pressure to the foot reflexes which relate to the symptoms. Unlike foot massage, the reflexologist does not use oil, since it makes problem areas in the foot more difficult to detect. The pressure on the reflex encourages your energy to flow through disturbed areas in a more balanced way.

The pressure on a reflex point sometimes causes sensitivity. This tenderness is an indication of congestion or weakness in the system. Pressing on tender reflex points sends energy to the organ, muscle or gland that needs help to break up wastes and send them to the proper organs of elimination.

Because reflexology occasionally causes pain, it is important to feel trusting of your practitioner. If your fear blocks the cycle of giving and receiving of energy, the treatment will not be as effective. A sensitive practitioner will also respect a client's indications that the pace of the treatment needs to be slower and gentler.

The health benefits of reflexology greatly outweigh any occasional pain. Since it improves the circulation, you will feel lighter, less tense, and tingly after a treatment. A series of treatments will strengthen and balance your entire system.

Reflexology, which sends energy through longitudinal channels, beautifully complements chiropractic care. Chiropractic adjustments open the energy channels of the spinal column to reestablish smooth communication between the central nervous system and the body along horizontal channels girdling the torso. Until these connections are restored, it is not possible for the body to fully regain health. If we could visualize the natural healing arts as a great tree, chiropractic care would be the trunk, while reflexology would be one of the branches.

Reiki

Reiki also originated in Japan, and is now practised around the world. Reiki practitioners gently facilitate the balancing of body, mind and spirit, offering a light touch through which a loving universal life energy flows. A reiki practitioner rests his or her hands at various places on your body. The specific places follow a special sequence. Sometimes the reiki practitioner will also rest the hands on painful or injured areas.

As the practitioner touches you, he or she channels universal healing energy through your system, which is used by you in the way it is most needed. Sometimes a reiki treatment will make you feel temporarily worse as strength gained pushes hidden problems into conscious awareness.

When we receive reiki we support our body's natural ability to heal itself, and we open the door to reestablishing well-being and smooth functioning on all levels: physical, emotional, mental and spiritual. Reiki also balances all our energies and promotes a state of total relaxation. It is a very pleasant wholistic healing method. Reiki can never do damage in any way. I have found it to be an excellent addition to a skin care program.

Everyone responds differently to reiki. You may feel a great spaciousness inside your being, and depths of inner peace and quiet. You may feel spontaneous sensations of happiness, or a simple, relaxing sense of balance. Many people also feel flowing sensations, often combined with feelings of warmth. You can experiment with reiki on your own by trying the exercises outlined at the end of the section on Chakras. (Fig. 4) These are basically reiki techniques.

If you give or receive reiki regularly, you will notice new resources developing within. Self-trust, wisdom, the power to remain centred and balanced at all times, and a growing conscious awareness of the interconnectedness of all aspects of life will open new doors to love, pleasure and accomplishment in your life.

Shiatsu Therapy

Shiatsu is a gentle form of acupressure therapy developed in Japan. It will help you to release accumulated stresses and tensions, whether caused by the demands of your daily activities or rooted in traumatic events of the past. Shiatsu also helps us restore the balance between the physical, emotional and spiritual aspects of our being.

The practitioner uses his or her fingers to apply deep and gentle pressure at specific points along the body. The points fall on lines that travel up and down the body, called meridians. The meridians correlate to the different organ systems in the same way the different areas of the face do. As the points are stimulated, energy blockages and weak energetic connections in the corresponding organs rebalance themselves. Thus the treatment promotes deep relaxation, strengthens the immune system and increases overall energy and vitality.

Shiatsu treatments are given on a soft mat on the floor. You may choose to wear loose, comfortable clothing during treatment or simply to be covered with a blanket. Frequency of treatment is based on individual needs. Some people schedule shiatsu on a regular basis to maintain their good health.

Therapeutic Environment

The environment you create for yourself is important in maintaining a positive and healthy attitude. The colours and music surrounding you colour your inner world. Why you prefer one colour over another, or one type of music over another at any given time has something to do with the way that colour or music makes you feel. Colour and music have enormous power to create changes in your being.

Pay attention to your clothing, to your home, to what is playing on the stereo. Do you enjoy your surroundings? Are they supportive of your mood? Of your current cycle of tasks? Your own intuition, if you take the time to ask yourself what you need when you get dressed in the morning or when you decide to play a cassette, will guide you effectively.

The following list may provide a good starting point for your own exploration and experimentation.

Red stimulates and warms the body.

Orange refreshes a fatigued state.

Yellow stimulates memory.

Green relaxes the whole body, mind and spirit. (Just think how pleasant plants make any space.)

Some wholistic practitioners you consult may use both coloured light and music as part of a treatment.

To conclude this chapter, I would like to encourage you. If you have not attempted a wholistic approach before, you may feel overwhelmed by your choices and unsure of your ability to judge wisely. Keep in mind that wholistic therapies always strengthen the system, and do not use toxic or invasive techniques. Any natural therapy you choose will leave you in a better condition to plan your next step. The important thing is to take action. Wholistic healing, by its very nature, cannot be understood without experiencing it.

Chapter Five

The Importance of Internal Cleansing

In Chapter 5, I begin my discussion of the specific components of Wholistic Facial Care. Because it is so important to the skin, internal cleansing is an essential element of the program.

In the preceding chapters we have seen over and over again that disturbances in balanced energy flow underlie illness of any kind. One of the most common ways in which we deny energy its freedom of movement is by neglecting to clean ourselves internally, as well as externally.

Think of what it is like to walk across a floor cluttered with objects, especially if you need to do it quickly. You have to step over things or walk around them, and your shoulders and neck will probably tense from the effort of making sure to see everything so you will not trip. The situation interferes with your balanced walking rhythm and blocks the smooth expression of your walking energy.

Most of us will not tolerate this type of situation for long in our outer surroundings. But a surprising number of us do not realize that our body and mind can grow cluttered as well. In the body, each living cell takes in nutrients and releases waste products continually. If the wastes are not eliminated, they accumulate. This then prevents the cells from being nourished properly and, as in a messy room, creates delays and detours in bodily functioning. In the mind, thoughts which weigh us down by creating unnecessary fears, angers, envies, and depression will quickly do the same to our mental and emotional functioning.

The skin is one of the four major organs of waste elimination in the body, along with the colon, kidneys and lungs. If we overload our inner self with waste, our eliminative energy, trying to do its work by any means possible, will bring the excess to the skin. This strategy might work on an occasional basis, but if our body must do this continually, the skin becomes overworked. The backlog of wastes can cause pimples, infections, blackheads or puffy, sagging, tired or discoloured skin. Such a situation also contributes to serious skin diseases such as acne, eczema and psoriasis.

When the skin shows such disorders, most people look for something to apply on the affected areas. However, the underlying cause of the problem is an interruption of the smooth functioning of the eliminative energy due to stress and overload of some type. This must be addressed before the skin can return to normal. A cleansing program combined with food therapy and proper dietary supplementation will stimulate the elimination of toxins and rebuild the balance of the whole system. Physical cleansing will encourage the growth of healthier mental attitudes. At the same time, physical cleansing will proceed much more effectively if we work to reorder our thought processes at the same time.

How Our Digestive Tract Works

Digestion turns food to energy, body building and repair materials and waste. Inefficient digestion results in larger amounts of waste, which in turn hamper digestion further and strain the eliminative organs, including the skin. Having a basic understanding of how the digestive tract works will help you to establish stronger digestion and to understand why I make the specific cleansing and dietary suggestions I do. The digestive tract is shown in Figure 6.

The description below follows the pathway of food through our bodies from the time we choose to eat it to the eventual elimination of the digested food from the colon.

1) *Mouth and Salivary Glands.* Digestion begins in the mouth. As the food is broken down by the teeth, a message to the brain instantly orders certain glands to deliver saliva. Saliva contains mainly water, mixed with mucus and enzymes needed to start the process of digestion.

Enzymes are chemicals which break food down into simple units that can be processed by our bodies. Some enzymes act on proteins, others on starches. The enzymes which break down starch exist mainly in the saliva. For this reason it is extremely important for us to chew our food well, mixing it thoroughly with saliva. Since the stomach cannot handle starches well, poorly chewed food will often

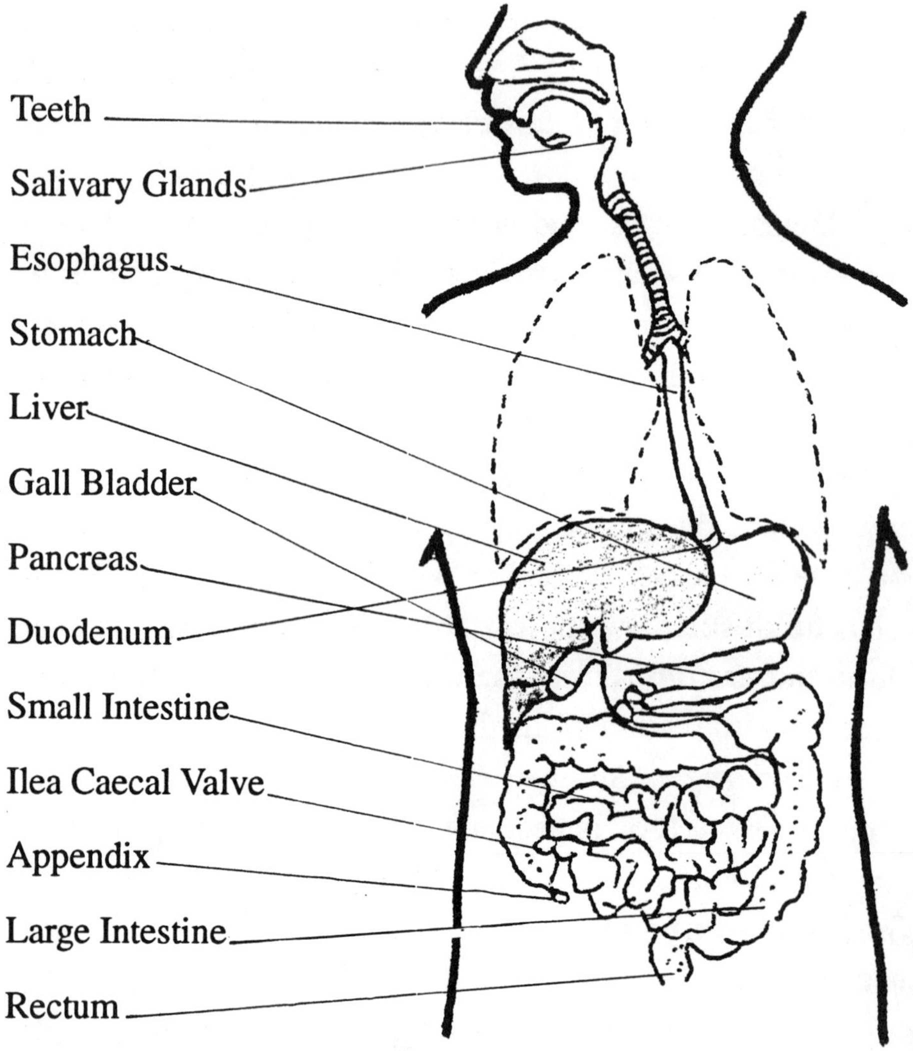

Figure 6. The Digestive System

stay in the stomach in an unprocessed state long enough to begin fermenting. Fermenting food produces toxins, and becomes compacted and unavailable to the body. As a result we may become full of gas, bloated and constipated.

We must consciously decide to chew in order to influence the activity of our saliva glands.

After we chew the food and mix it with saliva it is ready to be swallowed. The tongue helps the food along to the esophagus and stomach. The voluntary part of digestion ends here and automatic processes take over.

2) *Esophagus.* This tube leads from the mouth to the stomach. It dilates and contracts over and over again to move all the food swallowed into the stomach. Sometimes the muscle between the esophagus and stomach does not work properly. Acid from the stomach then enters the esophagus, causing "heartburn." Eating easily digestible food in a relaxed manner will keep this problem from occurring.

3) *Stomach.* The stomach is the largest muscular section of the digestive system. When we begin chewing food, the stomach prepares to further break it down by releasing acidic gastric juices and enzymes which act on proteins. The stomach is often our body's first line of defence against foods or combinations of foods we may not consciously know should be avoided. If something upsets your stomach, stop eating it, at least until your digestion is stronger. This simple precaution will powerfully safeguard your health.

4) *Small Intestine.* After it has mixed and broken down the food as thoroughly as possible, the stomach pumps it

into the small intestine. This tubular structure is approximately twenty-five feet long. Its size and the presence of millions of hairlike structures called villi ensure that a huge surface area interacts with the food. This gives us maximum contact with the nutrients we need, and also maximum contact with any toxins in the food.

The small intestine secretes a variety of digestive substances and also receives secretions from the pancreas, liver and gall bladder which help break down the food. Brief descriptions of the functions of the pancreas, gall bladder and liver follow.

5) *Pancreas.* The pancreas produces enzymes and other substances which work in the small intestine to extract the materials we need from our food. In addition to its role in digestion, the pancreas also acts as a gland, helping to regulate blood sugar levels.

6) *Gall Bladder.* The gall bladder stores bile, a substance produced by liver cells, and releases it for use in digestion when necessary. Bile contains cholesterol, inorganic salts and lecithin. Lecithin is an emulsifier, which means that it breaks down fats. If the bile contains too much cholesterol and not enough lecithin, gallstones may form.

The formation of gallstones can usually be avoided by eating a low fat, natural diet with plenty of foods rich in roughage.

7) *Liver.* The liver plays an enormous, crucial role in digestion. It performs hundreds of different types of biochemical operations daily. Its major function is to metabo-

lize proteins, carbohydrates and fats, converting them into the energy we need. The liver also works to detoxify or neutralize unneeded hormones, and eliminates toxins that have found their way into the blood, the large intestines and the kidneys. For this reason, people whose work regularly puts them in contact with poisonous chemicals often suffer liver damage and liver cancer. The liver also stores vitamins, minerals, proteins and glucose, for release into the body as needed. Finally, this amazing organ manufactures bile, which, as we have seen, is extremely important in the digestion of fats.

8) *Large Intestines (Colon).* After the small intestine has pushed the food through its biochemical factory, it enters the large intestines or colon. As the colon pushes the food through its length, it squeezes and reabsorbs excess water from the mash created in the small intestine, absorbs more nutrients from the food and eventually eliminates the waste products of digestion.

If the colon is sluggish, waste matter will putrefy inside it, eventually poisoning the whole body. In such conditions yeasts may also colonize the colon. Their metabolic by-products also poison the body.

If we maintain strong colon functioning, our eliminative energy will be able to rid our body of more deeply deposited wastes by bringing them to this organ. Fortunately it is not difficult to strengthen the colon. How to accomplish this will be discussed shortly.

We have now looked at the basic steps of digestion. This

process supplies our bloodstream with proteins needed for cell repair and reproduction, sugars for basic energy, fatty acids that we use to create our body's heat, and vitamins and minerals which regulate our metabolism.

9) *Consciousness.* The last, more complex element of digestion that must be considered is our consciousness. The digestive system is an elaborate mechanism coordinated and controlled by the nervous system. Thus, feelings of anger, fear, tension or insecurity easily and powerfully influence digestion. Keeping this in mind will prevent many digestive problems and your skin will glow as a result. Try not to eat when you are angry, experiencing an emotional shock, tired, or stressed. (Later in this chapter I will discuss a method for clearing unneeded anger, fear and tension from the mind.)

You may also find it helpful not to eat when you are sick. Allow your body to concentrate on freeing itself of disease instead. Make sure in this case to get plenty of liquids however, especially vegetable broths, which are rich in vitamins and minerals. In general, eat only when you feel hungry.

Remember to chew well. Eat in a peaceful atmosphere. Do not eat while standing, watching television, reading, or talking on the phone. Leave at least three hours between your last meal and bedtime. Digestion is inactive at night. You will see your mental, emotional and physical state show improvement.

In general, staying centred and calm will keep digestion strong. The importance of breathing deeply, no matter what our circumstances, cannot be overestimated with regard to this. We can also make sure to maintain our potassium levels, especially when we are facing higher levels of stress. The adrenal glands, just above the kidneys, are strongly affected by stress, and need more potassium in such a situation to function well. This gland plays an important role in keeping the entire system balanced. Nurture it by eating foods rich in potassium, especially when you are stressed. These include whole grains, broccoli, asparagus, avocado, raw carrots, cooked beans, steamed spinach, raw tomatoes, apples, bananas, cantaloupes, oranges, peaches and chicken, liver, cod, salmon and tuna.

Probably the most important thing we can do to establish a good relationship between our emotions and our digestion is to remember our gratitude for the food. Take a moment before each meal to demonstrate in your own way your thankfulness to the foods, and to their ultimate source, for the life and energy they give you. When you do this, you can enjoy and fully benefit from your meal, no matter what your outward circumstances are.

Internal Cleansing

Please keep in mind as you read this section that the guidelines I give here are general, and not tailored to individual needs. Keep an open mind not only to what you read here, but to your own experience.

1) *The Colon.* As shown earlier, strong colon functioning

supports the health of the whole body.

To improve the colon's eliminative abilities, take one tablespoon of psyllium powder mixed in a glass of water or juice each morning and evening. The psyllium will fill out the colon with a gelatinous mass. This acts as a very gentle laxative and also cleans the walls of the intestines as it is pushed along.

When you are just beginning to cleanse the colon, psyllium is a better choice than colonic irrigation. It works more gently and slowly. This reduces the chance of sudden dramatic releases of toxins, which may interrupt one's daily tasks. Psyllium also cleanses the small intestine as well as the colon, following the natural path of ingested food. Later, when your health is better established, colonic irrigation will be easily handled by your system.

The colon hosts bacteria which actually help us digest our food, and also keep yeast in check. These bacteria also depend on healthy colon functioning to create the living conditions they need. If the colon begins to fill with partially digested and fermenting foods, yeast will crowd out the bacteria. Antibiotics create the same problem. Yeast is a parasite which eats our food and adds it digestive wastes to the burden on our eliminative organs. When you begin to cleanse your colon, make sure to take acidophilus in tablet or liquid form to reestablish a healthy colonic ecology. Vitamins A and E are helpful in combination with the acidophilus.

Finally, exercise greatly benefits the colon. Walk or ride a bicycle to reach your destinations whenever possible. Do five sit-ups each day. If you want to be sure not to strain the lower back, you can also exercise the abdominal muscles by sitting supported by a wall and lifting your legs off the floor.

2) *Fasting.* Fasting effectively eliminates waste from our system and enhances the healing processes of the body. It gently clears up skin complaints. Fasting need not strain your endurance. There are many ways to fast, each meeting different needs and suited to different personalities. I prefer the gentler methods of fasting, and they are what I will describe here. To help you determine the method of fasting best suited to your situation, consult a naturopath.

The *morning fast* is the gentlest of all ways to fast, and can be safely and beneficially practised every day. To follow this fast, you simply delay breakfast by an hour or two each morning.

When you get up, simmer several slices of ginger root in a cup of water for six to eight minutes. Strain the ginger from the water and add the juice of half a lemon and if desired, any of a teaspoon of honey, a pinch of cayenne pepper and a pinch of cinnamon. This drink will start your stomach and gastric juices flowing. As there is no food for them to digest, however, they will break down anything left in the digestive tract from the day before and eventually, old, unprocessed wastes. Drinking this mixture also revitalizes blood circulation, assists blood cleansing, and helps clear phlegm and rheumatic infections from the chest and stomach.

An hour or two after drinking the ginger-lemon mixture, enjoy a light, easily digestible breakfast.

Experiment with following this routine daily. You should notice positive changes in your digestion within a week or two.

You can also use the ginger-lemon drink as an enjoyable substitute for alcoholic drinks.

In my experience, another gentle, effective fast is a *weekly fast.* This fast lasts for twenty-four hours, on the same day of each week. Eat no solid foods, but have all the liquids you want: broth, dandelion and chicory coffee, vegetable or fruit juices and spring water. (Do not mix fruit and vegetable juices however.) This fast gives your stomach a good rest.

The weekly fast should also be supported by nutritional supplements to avoid any harm. Take 1000 mg of vitamin C, 100 mg of niacin (vitamin B_3) and 50 mg of potassium two times during the fasting day. Vitamin C helps to detoxify poisons being released into the bloodstream. Niacin eliminates toxins from the capillaries. It causes a blushing sensation, but this is harmless and lasts only fifteen to thirty minutes, then disappears. The potassium assists the kidneys during the fast and helps the body to release excess salt.

The kidneys filter metabolic and toxic wastes from the blood and excrete them through the urethra in the form of urine. (Figure 7 shows the kidneys and bladder.) During the fast, support your kidneys by drinking large amounts of water. I usually recommend two glasses of pure water around the following times: eight and eleven o'clock in the morning, and two, five and eight o'clock in the afternoon and evening.

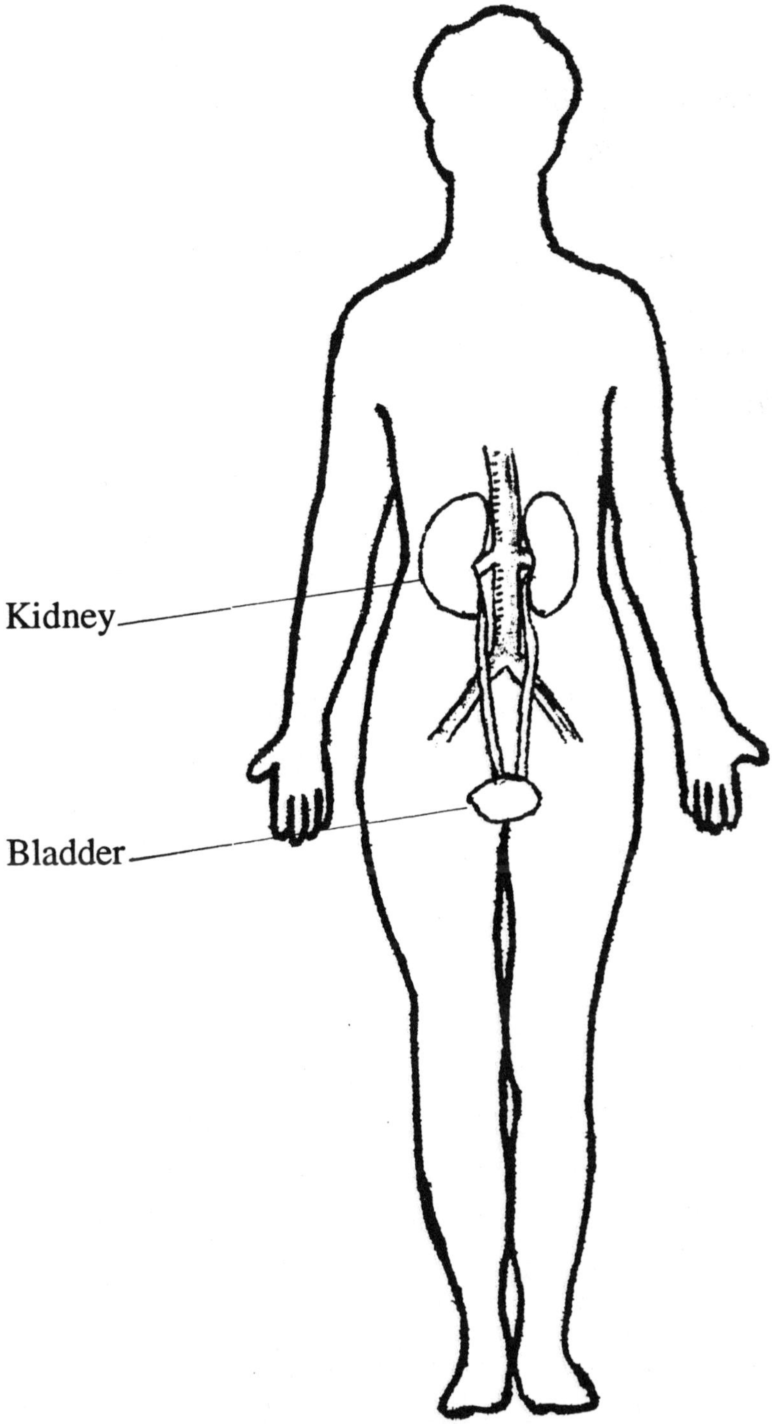

Figure 7. Kidneys and Bladder

Body temperature usually drops during the fast. Therefore it is important to keep yourself warm.

When you begin to eat again, make sure to chew very well and choose light, easily digestible foods in quantities smaller than usual for your first meal or two. A health supportive, easily digestible diet is outlined in the next chapter.

You may occasionally wish to reinforce the effects of the liquid fast by eating only fruit and fruit juice for two to three days after. Then resume one meal per day at lunch or dinner, and have fruit or fruit juice the rest of the day for another few days. It is helpful to complement this program with acidophilus capsules, lecithin and vitamin E capsules twice a day.

In temperate climates follow a fruit diet only in the summer. Otherwise you will cool yourself internally and lose resistance to the cold. If you have weak kidneys, as evidenced by consistently colourless urine or edema, you will do best to avoid a fruit-based diet. Use cooked vegetables and vegetable broth with some sea vegetables added as the basis of a cleansing diet.

As you follow a fasting and dietary program suitable for you, you will find yourself gradually and easily losing weight if you need to. You will find it easier to eliminate solid food, and the process of detoxification will be evident in the changing texture of your skin.

I would like to end the section on fasting with one final caution. Even the short morning fast described earlier can be difficult at first for someone who suffers from hypoglycemia (low blood sugar.) Eventually, it will help to heal this condition however. If you do suffer from hypoglycemia, you can try beginning with a very short morning fast, ten, twenty or thirty minutes in length. Your strength will build quickly. Make sure too that you are strong enough before attempting the weekly fast, epecially if you plan to work as usual on the fast day. Seek out a qualified naturopath for assistance and guidance if you feel any doubts. Diabetics should not attempt any type of fasting without medical approval and supervision.

Continued Cleansing

We can continue the cleansing process while eating normally and going about our daily activities.

Regularly drinking freshly pressed raw vegetable or fruit juices has a remarkable cleansing and energizing effect on the whole body. Some juice combinations are particularly helpful for certain organs. In the juice combinations listed below, the proportions of each vegetable are up to your individual taste. Drink these juices with a meal, or as dessert. Taken before a meal, their unadulterated power may upset your stomach. If you want to receive full benefit from these juices, always drink them immediately after making them.

The following juice combinati ons help to heal the colon and to restore deficiencies in adrenal secretions to the entire intestinal tract:

1) *spinach, lettuce, watercress, carrots, green pepper*
2) *parsley, spinach, celery, lettuce*
3) *parsley, carrot, cucumber*

The next juice combination is an overall tonic. It cleanses and strengthens the liver, kidneys, stomach and blood:

dandelion leaves, parsley, carrot

For liver trouble, try juice of *dandelion leaves* diluted with water and sweetened with *honey*, several glasses per day.

For gallstones, a combination of *beet juice* and *lemon juice* taken several times per day with plenty of water, over the course of two or three weeks, will help to dissolve the stones. Other stronger natural remedies to flush out gallstones exist. You should use these only on the advice of a naturopath. Their effects are too powerful for unsupervised use.

If you suffer from rheumatism, try a mixture of juices from the following vegetables:

beet, carrot, cucumber, parsley, celery, dandelion

Finally I offer a list of six juices which help to revitalize the body's functioning and have been used to help the following conditions: acne, anemia, arthritis, bladder trouble, colds, constipation, dizziness, eczema, fatigue, gout, hair and scalp problems, headaches, indigestion, insomnia, itching, kidney troubles, menopausal difficulties, migraines, nervousness, obesity, pneumonia, psoriasis and toxemia.

Again, your own intuitions and the help of a qualified wholistic doctor can aid you in deciding which of these juices is needed at a given time:

1) *carrot, beets, cucumber, parsley, dandelion*
2) *carrot, celery, parsley, cucumber, lemon*
3) *spinach, parsley, broccoli, carrot, celery*
4) *parsley, asparagus, lettuce, carrot, spinach, broccoli*
5) *garlic, beet, parsley, green pepper, cucumber, celery*
6) *carrot, beet, broccoli, celery, cucumber, kale, lettuce, spinach*

Vegetable and fruit juices should not be taken together as they are very difficult to digest in combination. This is discussed in more detail in the next chapter. Take the following fruit juice on its own then. It helps to generally strengthen digestion.

Make a puree of banana, guava, mango or papaya. Mix this puree with other fresh fruit juices. You can choose among so many fruits: apple, apricot, grape, grapefruit, orange, peach, pear, pineapple, or others to your taste. The combination of pureed fruit and other juices makes a substantial, tasty drink. Remember that fruit suits summer best, and do not overdo it. We need other foods for lasting stamina.

Another excellent and pleasurable technique for continuing the cleansing process in daily life is the sauna.

Taking a sauna increases your metabolic rate, and boosts the circulation of the blood and the lymph fluids, an important part of our disease fighting mechanism. When the circulation of these body liquids speeds up, their ability to remove toxins increases. Sweat, also encouraged by the sauna, then carries the toxins completely out of the body through the skin.

Cleansing the Mind

If we cleanse our bodies but neglect our minds, we miss an opportunity for deeper healing. Habitual anger, fear, depression, anxiety and alienation all profoundly harm our health, and in the long run can cause serious physical illness. If we work to liberate the mind of unneeded negative thoughts and emotions at the same time as we work to cleanse the body, each effort will also support and strengthen the progress of the other. In this way, we give ourselves a doorway to a happier day-to-day life.

Making sure to take time to listen to your own spirit regularly, as I have outlined in Chapter 3, will help you to maintain clear mental and emotional functioning. Your responses will remain appropriate to the situation.

Deep breathing also keeps the mind and emotions functioning as they should.

Cognitive behaviour therapy is also very valu… within a wholistic approach. This therapy heals mental and emotional problems without using drugs. Instead it teaches a method for releasing self-defeating mental habits and developing more effective models of thinking. It is possible to recreate our thinking processes so they support, rather than hinder, our progress towards our goals.

One of the basic ideas in cognitive therapy is that our thoughts create our feelings. How we think about the events in our life will in large part determine how we feel about them. We can avoid unnecessary negative feelings by changing our thought patterns.

It may not seem obvious that our thoughts create our feelings, but this is largely true. This explains why two people might respond to the same event in very different ways. For instance,one person may feel very happy that holidays are on the way, because they think they will receive many presents. Another person may feel depressed about the oncoming holiday, because they think they are incapable of choosing the right presents for anyone. Another might feel angry about upcoming holidays because they think other people always get better presents than they do. Granted, the people I am describing here are a little childish, but I believe I am making my point.

A person with a balanced approach to life and healthy self-esteem will trust his or her ability to choose the right presents, and knows that his or her worth does not depend on what presents arrive or do not arrive from others. This person is in the best position to flow with events as they arise and to respond appropriately.

Cognitive therapy has developed numerous techniques that help us maintain this inner balance in any situation. We then prevent a build-up of emotional tensions and gain control of unneeded and therefore unhealthy emotions that previously controlled us.

Difficult moments and temptations can be overcome when we refuse to increase our hardship with unhelpful thoughts. This sometimes requires a struggle, but it can be done. Making the effort will help rejuvenate your innate healing mechanism, and will restore health and energy to the whole body.

Luckily, cognitive therapy does not have to be expensive. You can learn the techniques yourself by reading and working through *The Feeling Good Handbook* by David Burns, M.D. (Plume, 1990; first published by William Morrow and Company, New York, 1989.) Doing so will cleanse, refresh and strengthen your mind and emotions. The results will show in your appearance. Your eyes and skin will reflect your new serenity and vitality.

Conclusion

Approached at the right pace, physical internal cleansing takes about a year. Keeping the process slow keeps it safe. Mental and emotional cleansing should also be approached slowly. Changes in thought patterns inevitably lead to changes in one's outer circumstances. Going at your own pace in this area will ensure that you are ready for the changes.

During the cleansing process you may occasionally experience signs of cleansing, such as nausea, indigestion, diarrhea or headaches. These occur when a larger amount of toxins than usual are being pushed out of the body. If such symptoms last more than a few days however, consult a wholistic physician, as you may have contracted a more serious illness.

As with all the wholistic therapies, the long term benefits of internal cleansing far outweigh the temporary difficulties. You will gain energy and vitality, lower your risk of degenerative disease and cancer, and find it easier to stay balanced and happy within your relationships and daily circumstances.

Chapter Six

A Daily Routine

Wholistic healers really can perform wonders at times, and the techniques of internal cleansing will always be powerfully health supportive. But is it useful to invest time, energy and money in work with a wholistic practitioner if your daily habits work against the healing you receive? Is it sensible to clean up a mess if your daily lifestyle continually recreates it?

This chapter outlines my suggestions for a daily routine which supports health and healing. Again, use these suggestions in combination with the guidance of your own intuition and experience. Remember there will be some effort involved in changing your habits. But once you establish new routines, they do not take more energy than your old ones. In fact, they provide you with energy, whereas unhealthy habits drain vitality.

If you combine a daily routine which promotes your health and happiness with the use of *Leahder* (details are given in Chapter 7) and the healing techniques outlined in Chapters 4 and 5, you will be rewarded with beautiful, smoothly textured skin, as well as increased vigour for life.

Following are my suggestions for a happy, fulfilling lifestyle.

Breathing

I have already discussed breathing in Chapter 4, but I feel I cannot emphasize the importance of good breathing enough.

Breathing is life.

Life begins with breathing and ends with breathing. Oxygen is one of the major nutrients for the whole system, the other being water. Every breath exerts influence over our mental, emotional and physical state, helping to keep us in harmony. Consciously choose to breathe deeply as often as you can and remember to use your breath as a support for all other activities.

Taking regular breaks to do breathing exercises such as the ones described later in this chapter will ensure that you stay in touch with your spiritual centre. This is the part of you that knows where you are going and how you can best respond to any situation.

Food: Your Daily Healer

We move through life by eating. Through our food we receive the sun, water, heat, cold, dryness and wetness. Our own nature integrates the properties of the food we eat.

Not everyone will benefit equally from the same food. To establish your own dietary needs, observe how you feel after eating specific foods or combinations of foods. Pay attention to how various foods affect your digestion. Does a specific food improve your overall functioning, or does it interfere with your well-being? Try new foods and combinations of foods often, carefully observing their effects, and you will most likely discover foods that increase your level of well-being. If you read or hear of a new diet that appeals to you, try it. But do not hesitate to drop it if you do not enjoy it or if it does not show any results by one month.

There are general guidelines with respect to food which you can use to keep your dietary experimentation within safe limits.

We all need to eat food which provides us with essential nutrients. Proteins help us create and repair body tissues. We need carbohydrates for an energy source. Fats store energy and cushion the internal organs. We need essential fatty acids to keep certain metabolic processes going. Vitamins and minerals are essential to biochemical functions. Make sure to eat a wide variety of foods from all the categories listed in the food combining chart (Figure 8) and you will guarantee a healthful supply of all these nutrients.

Fibre is also an important component of the diet. Fibre encourages complete digestion and efficient elimination of waste. Good fibre sources include cooked cabbage, cooked carrots, raw apples, pears and bananas, whole grains, whole grain flours and bran. In general, foods in their whole form, as nature gives them to us, are a far superior starting point for meals than canned, frozen, deep-fried, milled, bleached and overly processed foods. Eating foods from the area in which you live will improve your overall harmony with your environment, making life easier.

Keep fat consumption low and avoid animal fats especially. Cold pressed vegetable oils, available at health food stores will guard your health. These oils may seem expensive, but they should be used in small quantities. One bottle will go a long way.

Combining and Steaming Food

How we prepare and serve our food is just as important as what we eat. As we saw in Chapter 5, strong digestion is essential to good health. Eating incorrect combinations of food weakens digestion and allows partially digested food to remain and ferment in the digestive tract, eventually poisoning the blood. This happens because we need different enzymes to digest different types of food. If we eat foods at one meal which require different enzymes, they will interfere with one another and digestion will be much less efficient. In fact, improper food combining can cause severe stomach upsets. For your stomach, trying to deal with very different digestive demands at once is much like trying to participate in two or three separate conversations at once. Much is missed, and confusion and discomfort accompany the effort.

Combining foods intelligently detoxifies the blood and thereby reduces stress on the body. If your digestion is strong, correct food combining will keep it that way. If it is weak, good food combining will improve it. On pages 82 and 83 you will find a food combining chart that explains the principles involved.

Overcooking food drains it of its life-giving nutrients. Steaming food until it is just tender, and in the case of vegetables, still brightly coloured, ensures that food will be very digestible, nutritious and tasty. This method of cooking preserves vitamins and minerals which would otherwise be lost in cooking water. It keeps the food free of toxins and indigestible chemicals produced when oil is heated for frying. Eating steamed food regularly helps prevent cholesterol build-up in the body as well. Each steamed meal adds strength to health.

With curiosity, patience, a few utensils and some basic information, you can begin experimenting with steamed food. New mealtime pleasures will reward your efforts. To steam food you need a large pot with a layer of boiling water on the bottom. You also need a holder for the food which keeps it above the boiling water and allows the steam inside the pot to cook the food. The pot lid should fit well, otherwise the water in the bottom of the pot will boil away too quickly. Prevent scorched pots and lengthy cooking times by using a heavy, snug lid.

You can choose between Chinese bamboo steamers or American stainless steel leaf steamers. Bamboo steamers are usually designed to fit into special earthenware pots which do double duty as cooking vessels and serving dishes, for they retain heat and help keep the food warm at the table. Bamboo steamers often come as stacked sets. The round, shallow containers fit into one another so that as many as five different dishes can be steamed at once.

Leaf steamers are made of a circular base surrounded by

Non-Vegetarian Protein

•Beef liver

•Brain

•Crab

•Herring

•Mackerel

•Meats

•Ocean Fish

•Sardines

Oils

•Flax

•Olive

•Sesame

Vegetarian Protein

•Beans:

Azuki beans

Black beans

Kidney beans

Lentils

Mung beans

Pinto beans

Soy beans

•Cottage Cheese

•Tempeh,

•Tofu

•Yogurt

Guidelines

Do not eat non-vegetarian protein at the same meal with vegetarian protein or cereals.

Non-vegetarian proteins or vegetarian proteins combine well with vegetables.

Vegetarian protein combines well with cereals.

Oils can be eaten with any of the above correct combinations.

Fruits should be eaten on their own. Fruits can be mixed, except for melons, which should be eaten alone as well.

Figure 8. Food Combining Chart

Vegetables
- •Artichokes
- •Asparagus
- •Beets
- •Cabbage
- •Carrots
- •Cauliflower
- •Celery
- •Chard
- •Collards
- •Cucumber
- •Eggplant
- •Green Beans
- •Kale
- •Leeks
- •Lettuce
- •Peas
- •Potatoes
- •Radish
- •Sea Vegetables
- •Spinach
- •Squash
- •Tomatoes
- •Watercress

Grains
- •Amaranth
- •Barley
- •Bran
- •Buckwheat
- •Corn
- •Kamut
- •Millet
- •Oats
- •Quinoa
- •Rice
- •Rye
- •Spelt
- •Wheat

Guidelines

Do not drink with meals as the liquid washes away the salivary juices which are so essential in assisting the digestion of foods. Drink before or after meals.

In my observation, bitter food helps elimination. Spicy food activates cleansing and warms the body.

Avoid alcohol, strong tea and coffee. Tobacco smoking should be cut down.

Figure 8. Food Combining Chart

"leaves" which fold up and down. Leaf steamers are easier to clean than bamboo steamers, and very inexpensive. They fold out or in to fit the pots you already have.

Cooking times when steaming food are generally quite short, often only ten to fifteen minutes. You can steam whole grains, beans, noodles, vegetables, fish, poultry, meat and fruits. It is best to soak whole grains and beans in water overnight before steaming them. These foods will also take longer to cook. They should be soft and sweet tasting when done.

To enrich the flavour of steamed foods, put herbs which traditionally complement the food you are preparing in the cooking water. You can also add ginger and lemon juice to the cooking water. Or try spreading lemon juice and herbs over the food for two hours before you steam it. With time, you will find yourself creating many new dishes full of rich, natural flavour.

Daily Diet

On a daily basis, I eat one steamed meal at lunch or dinner which combines either a vegetarian or non-vegetarian protein with plenty of vegetables. I start the day with a puree of banana, mango, papaya or guava, mixed with other fruit juices, or I eat yogurt mixed with banana or mango. The rest of the day I consume liquids, fresh fruits or raw vegetables. I recommend taking water at eight and eleven o'clock in the morning, and two, five and eight o'clock in the afternoon and evening. On this diet I have no health complaints.

People living in cold climates, people who work hard physically, and those suffering from degenerative illness, weak kidneys or diabetes should avoid large amounts of fruit and raw foods and eat more heavy, cooked foods such as grains, beans, vegetables, fish and soups. Sea vegetables are especially helpful for strengthing the kidneys, sexual organs, teeth, hair and fingernails.

Whatever your diet, it is best to start the day with lighter foods and progress to heavier foods at lunch and dinner.

If you have never paid attention to your diet before, remember that it will take time to become comfortable with changes you make. Try to shift to a healthier life-style gradually, and if you indulge in foods you know are unhealthy for you, do not feel guilty about it. In time unhealthy foods and junk foods will simply lose their appeal, with no special effort on your part needed.

I would like to conclude this section on "Daily Diet" with an introduction to healing properties I have found everyday foods to have. Again I emphasize that not everyone responds to the same foods in the same way. If something on this list helps you, that is good. If your intuition suggests further reading or research is needed, trust yourself.

Except for celery, the foods on the following list have the properties indicated in their steamed form.

Artichoke: helpful in cases of diabetes, rheumatism and obesity.

Asparagus: diuretic properties.

Brussel sprouts: rich in protein, and when steamed and taken in moderation, helpful for digestive disorders.

Carrots: of great value, prevent cataracts.

Celery: helps rheumatism and also benefits nervous disorders. Best eaten raw.

Cucumber: good for rheumatism and for build-up of uric acid. Acts as a blood cleaner.

Grapefruit: improves digestion; corrects rheumatic disorders and relieves constipation.

Lemon: helps prevent colds.

Oranges: purify the blood, and relieve constipation. Should be avoided by people who suffer from sluggish livers.

Potatoes: for anemia.

Rhubarb: for stomach complaints, and to ease build-up of uric acid.

The Aging Process

Those of us over thirty must take our increasing age into account when planning a daily health routine. At this age, the immune system begins to slow down, and, though only very subtly at first, the digestion begins to weaken. Our metabolism begins to slow down as well. Cells receive fuel and wastes are eliminated less efficiently. Therefore the importance of taking dietary supplements increases with age. Enriching the supply of nutrients to the system will slow down the degenerative processes that accompany aging.

If you are over thirty, I recommend the following supplements to support cell activity and cell reproduction: vitamin C, 1000 mg, two times per day, vitamin E, 400 mg, two times per day and Selenium, 100 mg, once a day.

I also recommend a multi-vitamin and mineral tablet once a day, especially when you get older.

If you are a woman, supplementing your diet with calcium in the years before menopause will help ensure that you do not develop brittle and deformed bones late in life. A diet low in animal products and high in grains, beans, sea vegetables, (a very rich natural source of calcium) and vegetables will also help keep your bones strong.

Consult a naturopath for in-depth information on supplementation as it relates to your needs.

Protecting Yourself from Environmental Contaminants

In Chapter 2, I discussed the fact that environmental pollutants injure our health and our skin. Our daily diet and lifestyle can significantly reduce the potential harmful effects of environmental irresponsibility.

Whenever possible, shop at health food stores for certified organically grown foods. These are grown without hormones, antibiotics, pesticides, herbicides, and chemical fertilizers, which are all poisons to living beings. Organic foods taste much better than conventionally grown food and they really do make a difference to your health.

Drink spring water or filtered water. Chlorine is toxic, and many municipal water supplies contain many other poisonous chemicals as well.

Plant trees around your home and keep green plants in the house to filter the air.

Use electrical appliances only as necessary and avoid electric blankets or other long lasting exposures to strong electromagnetic fields. Electrical appliances and high voltage power lines seriously interfere with the electrical and magnetic energies that function in our own bodies. They inhibit our ability to fight cancer.

Because the ozone layer has been so seriously depleted by chemicals, many more ultra-violet rays from the sun reach our skin nowadays. I believe skin needs the sunlight. However, I recommend exposing your skin to the sun only when its energy is gentle. Allow the sun to touch your face before ten o'clock in the morning and after four o'clock in the afternoon. Even at those times you may decide you want to use sun screen and/or a hat.

Eating a small amount of cooked sea vegetables every day (arame, dulse, hijiki, kelp, kombu) will clean your body of radioactive poisons and toxic heavy metals such as mercury, lead and cadmium.

Avoid using toxic chemicals to clean your home. Stick to natural soaps, baking soda for scouring and vinegar for wiping floors. Your surroundings both indoors and in the lakes and rivers in your area will be better for it.

Finally, you may wish to consider how you can help create a new consciousness in the human race. When we truly love ourselves, we will no longer find it acceptable to poison the air, water and soil on which we depend. Until that day, no life form on earth is safe from the devastating effects of environmental damage.

Personal Cleanliness

You can easily assist your body to rid itself of wastes and toxins, whether they are by-products of digestion or environmental pollutants. This is done by thorough regular washing of areas where we naturally eliminate wastes. Not only the skin and hair but also the eyes, tongue, teeth, nasal passages, stomach and bowels should be kept clean.

Clean your tongue each morning, or even better, each evening. Rub it from the back to the front with your fingers or a toothbrush and a little water. Then rinse your mouth and spit out the water.

To cleanse your nasal passages, put water that has been mixed with a little baking soda or salt in a bowl. Then inhale the water from the bowl and sneeze it out again. This technique works most effectively if you sneeze out the water one nostril at a time, by holding the other one down with your finger. If any of the liquid runs down to your throat, you may find the sensation peculiar, but no harm will be done. The salt or soda will simply disinfect the nose and throat passages. Nasal cleansing is best done in the morning.

I have already described the weekly twenty-four hour fast in Chapter 5. This cleanses the stomach.

The bowels can be cleansed using psyllium, colonic irrigation or enemas. For information on psyllium, see Chapter 5, for information on colonic irrigation, see Chapter 4. If you choose to give yourself enemas at home, I recommend the following schedule. Take one enema per week for a month, then one enema every two weeks in the next month. Finally, take only one enema in the third month. After that you may find it helpful to take a series of four or five enemas each spring and fall. Remember to supplement your diet with acidophilus to replace lost digestive bacteria whenever you take colonic irrigations or enemas.

The cleansing practices listed here will strengthen your resistance to disease and infection.

Relaxation and Stretching

I recommend stretching and relaxation exercises as an excellent activity to do before and after a morning workout or before going to sleep in the evening. Stretching and relaxation exercises keep us feeling well and promote flexibility of both body and mind. I strongly recommend that you stretch frequently especially if you suffer from stiff muscles or regularly spend many hours sitting or working in one position. Stretching can also release emotional tensions locked in the muscles. This clears the way for energy to circulate in our bodies in a healthy, normal pattern.

Many resources exist to assist you with stretching. I will describe some of my favourite relaxation and stretching exercises a little later in this section. You may also find enjoyment and useful information through the exploration of yoga, tai chi, or dance.

I myself have practised yoga for many years.

Yoga originated in India and involves movement, stretching, breathing and meditation techniques. Beginners should always study yoga with a qualified teacher. It is too easy to make potentially dangerous errors when learning yoga postures from books.

Yoga educates the body through relaxed and graceful movements, stimulates the lungs and induces deep breathing, develops strength and muscle tone, improves blood circulation, breaks up calcium deposits in the body and lubricates the joints. Yoga also greatly benefits the central nervous system and contributes to longevity.

It takes only four weeks of consistent practice before a student of yoga begins to notice the positive effects: greater clarity of mind, a more energetic and relaxed approach to life, the disappearance of minor ailments, and the recovery of natural abilities to sleep deeply, digest food well, and eliminate wastes efficiently. Yoga brings joy to the heart, peace to the mind and health to the body.

The art of tai chi originated thousands of years ago in China, where millions of people still practise it daily. Practising tai chi involves making a series of slow, graceful movements which flow into one another, and stretch all the muscles and meridians. (See Shiatsu, Chapter 4.) The movements strengthen the organs, calm the mind and increase the student's general level of vitality. Tai Chi is also best learned from a teacher.

Whether you decide to pursue one of the Eastern movement arts or a Western dance form depends on your needs and personality. Stretching and moving are really so natural to us that you can invent your own ways too. Following are some of my favourite stretching and relaxation exercises to help you get started.

The best stretching is slow and gentle. Stretch your body lovingly and with pleasure in its movements, the way a purring cat does. Try to stretch further and further only very gradually, and do not force yourself to stretch if you feel tired and unwilling. You should enjoy each exercise. If you feel pain doing any movement, stop immediately.

A stretching session should last about fifteen to twenty minutes. Make sure to warm your muscles before you begin with a few moments of vigorous exercise, such as jogging in place. Repeat each exercise two or three times. Always relax in between exercises. Come out of all poses very slowly.

Flexibility varies from person to person. It may take months before you notice improvements in your own flexibility, but if you keep stretching you will. A daily practice will also contribute to constant progress towards harmonious development on the physical, emotional, mental and spiritual levels of your being.

Begin your stretching session with relaxation, then continue with more active exercises.

1) *Relaxation Exercise - Figure 9*

Sit on the floor with your legs spread apart, then bend your right knee to place the right foot touching the left inner thigh (groin). Then bring the left foot to the right groin area (tailor fashion). Place your hands on your knees, palms up, and straighten the spine so that the chest is held out, the abdomen in. Your torso should feel well balanced.

Hold your head erect with the chin parallel to the floor. Breathe deeply, quiet your mind, and concentrate on one simple, loving thought. Do this for one minute at a time at first. With practice, you will be able to hold this posture for longer periods of time.

Figure 9. Relaxation Exercise

2) *Stretching the Eyes - Figure 10*

Stretching the muscles which support the eyes benefits the nervous system. To stretch your eyes, look up while facing straight ahead and hold your eyes in this position for a few seconds. Then, in the same way, look to one side with both eyes. Then down, then to the other side. Repeat, moving in the opposite direction. Finally, make continuous circles in one direction, then the other, with both eyes at once.

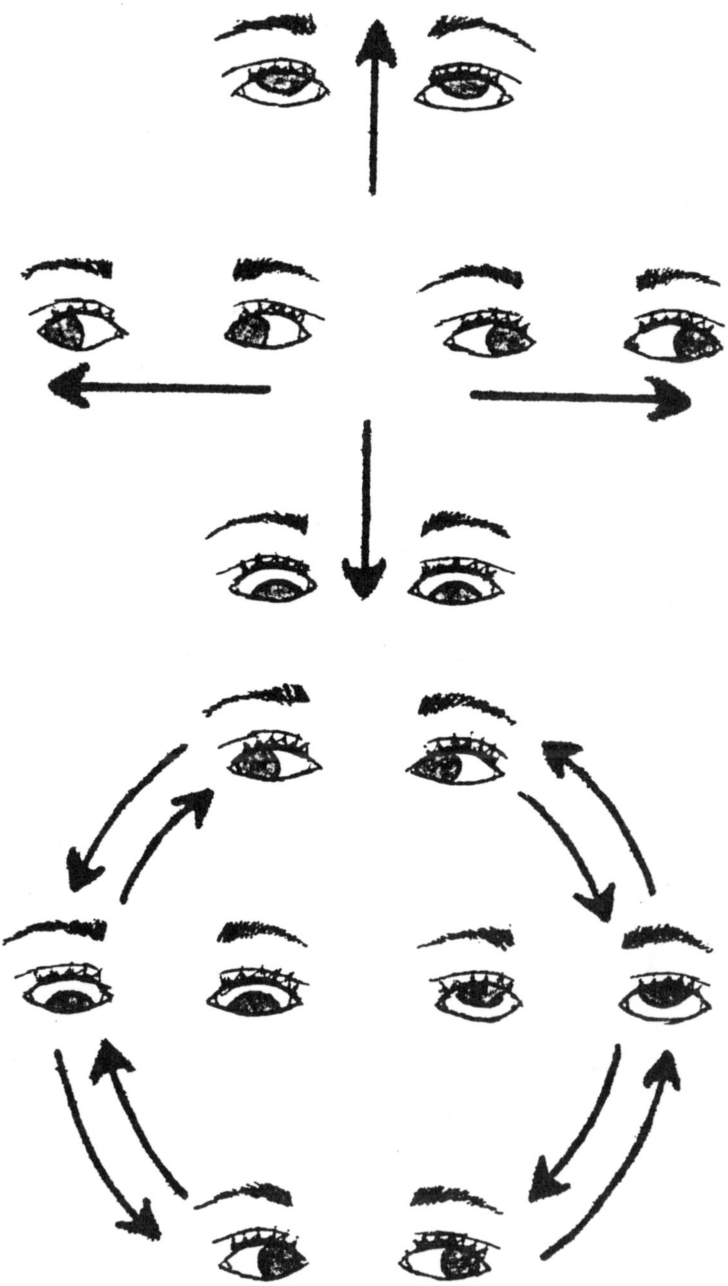

Figure 10. Stretching the Eyes

3) *Stretching Exercise - Figure 11*

This exercise helps you gain increased control of your back. It also strengthens the back and tones the kidneys, adrenal glands and thyroid.

Lie face down, your forehead on the floor, and place your palms on the floor close to your shoulders. Move your head so that your chin touches the floor, then move as far forward as possible without moving your hands. Now exhale, push down on your hands and curve your torso back, as though you were a cobra, one vertebrae after another, until the tension reaches your lumbar region, the area of your back opposite your loins. Keep your head forward, don't try to exaggerate the curve of the neck. Keep your gluteal muscles (your rear) tight to support the lower back.

Hold this position for six seconds, then let your head slowly drop forward and curve your spine in reverse order (starting with the lower back) to return to the floor. Exhale as you return to a lying position.

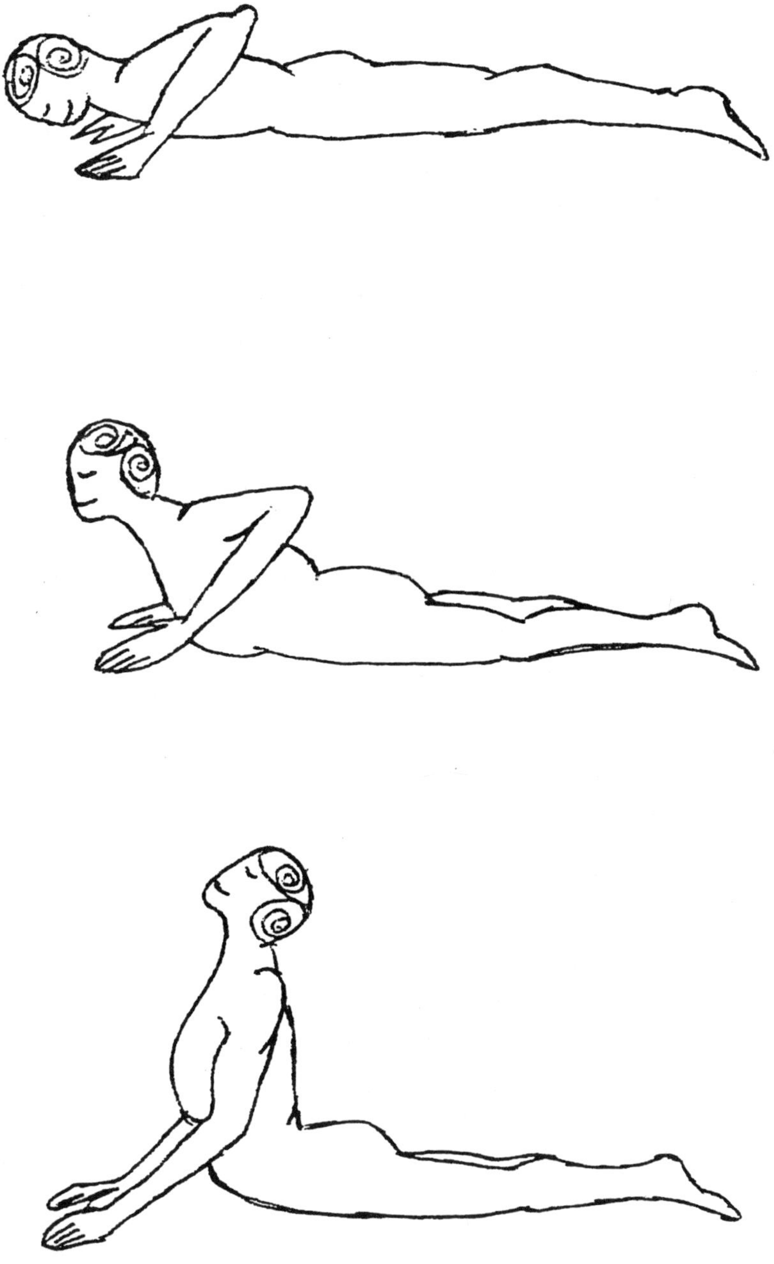

Figure 11. Stretching Exercise

2) *Stretching Exercise - Figure 12*

This exercise stretches the spine and the tendons and muscles of the legs. It also gives an internal massage to the heart and tones the entire body.

Sit with your legs straight out in front of you, with the chin parallel to the floor. While exhaling, lean forward as far as possible, extending your hands out to your feet. Then grasp your toes with your fingers and pull your head to your knees and your elbows to the floor. Try to keep the backs of your knees on the floor. Hold this position for a few seconds and then return to a sitting position very slowly.

Over a few months, gradually increase the amount of time you hold the posture to one minute.

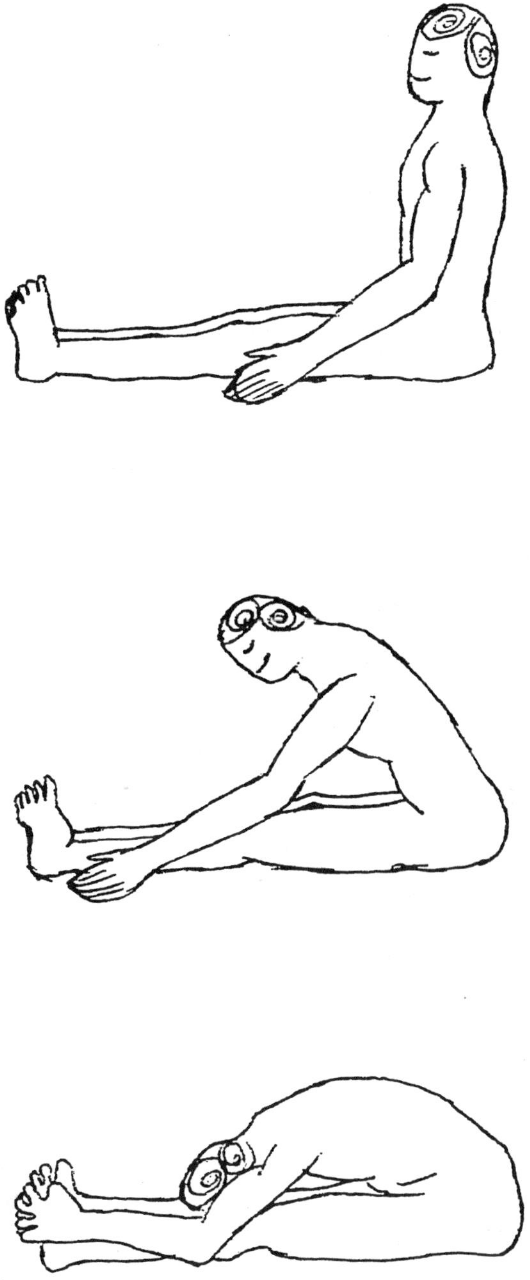

Figure 12. Stretching Exercise

End your stretching session with deep relaxation.

4) *Relaxation exercise - Figure 13*

Lie on the floor, eyes closed, heels together, toes apart, hands by your sides, shoulders flat. Begin to take deep, slow breaths. Select a number which suits you, and count to that number on the incoming breath, the held breath, the exhaled breath and the pause before the next breath. Each part of your breathing will thus be of the same length. Once you have a rhythm established, mentally relax the following areas of your body: toes, ankles, knees, thighs, anus, reproductive organs, navel, heart, neck, lips, tip of the nose.

To breathe in such a way balances the opposing and complementary energies in your being and also balances the nervous system. It revitalizes the blood and increases the energy of your chakras along the spine. Holding the breath oxygenates the blood and stimulates the lungs.

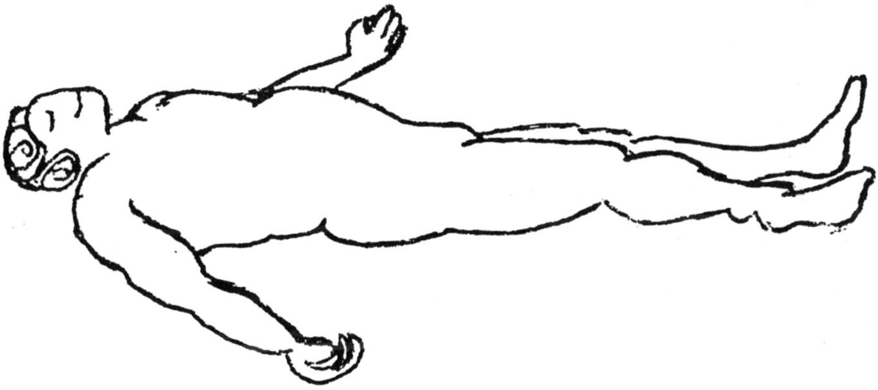

Figure 13. Relaxation Exercise

Creative Fulfillment

Health for its own sake quickly becomes a chore. What do you want to accomplish, to create in your life? If you do not work towards your creative goals regularly, you will likely experience depression and alienation from yourself. Let your healing work support your creative vision.

Creative work, in its turn, supports our healing process because success demands we balance our interior process and exterior work. Self-exploration and inner growth inspire creative projects. The outer work in its turn inspires self-reflection and evaluation. The inner and outer processes nourish each other. If we focus exclusively on outward accomplishments, we will seriously deplete our inner life, including the internal life of the body. If we only think and dream we will deplete our ability to accomplish our goals. Flexibility, moderation in all things and sensitivity to your own pace and needs will keep you strong. You will then be able to achieve everything you want from life.

In Conclusion: To Maintain Good Health

Keep your bowels moving. (Keep your colon clean.)

Keep your body moving. (Exercise regularly.)

Keep your breath moving, slowly and deeply.

Overcome evil with good, cruelty with kindness, ignorance with wisdom.

Celebrate the beauty of life.

Participate creatively with your fellow humans in the

cycle of giving and receiving.

Hug and be hugged often. It does wonders for the metabolism.

Be open to change. It always brings joy.

Let love, rather than fear, guide your way.

Chapter Seven

Treatment Methods in Wholistic Facial Care

If you have been reading this book in the order in which it is presented, you are now familiar with a wide range of information that will help you establish vibrant health and beauty.

You may however wish to receive help and guidance in creating a personalized beauty oriented health program. It is often easier to access greater healing energy when working within a trusting and comfortable relationship with another. A certified Wholistic Facial Care practitioner may be the person you want to work with.

You will find consultation with a practitioner especially helpful if you suffer from severe skin problems such as acne, psoriasis, or eczema. Such illnesses can often be quite stubborn and require patience and perseverance. The support and encouragement of a trained therapist can be of immense value as you may easily become discouraged if you have to work all alone.

You may also find much of the information in this chapter, especially the description of a facial with *Leahder,* helpful to your own health and beauty program whether or not you choose to work with a Wholistic Facial Care practitioner.

Wholistic Facial Care can also provide you with an exciting career, full of creative challenge. If you are interested in becoming a practitioner, please contact the Natural Healing Service at the address given at the back of this book.

Wholistic Facial Care: An Overview

Wholistic Facial Care offers a pleasurable route to beauty, deep relaxation and health improvement all at the same time. It is capable of healing even very damaged skin by working with the body, not against it.

The techniques and substances used in Wholistic Facial Care remove dead cells from the surface of the skin and provide a complete food supply to the living skin cells. The process stimulates lasting changes in skin texture and eliminates unbalanced skin conditions. Smell, sound and colour therapy and food therapy enhance the fundamental treatment of the skin with *Leahder.*

1) *Leahder. Leahder*, a series of products of my own invention, consists of natural, active lotions and essential oils. *Leahder* is completely non-toxic. In fact, *Leahder* is food for the skin. The products penetrate and feed damaged skin, helping to restore biological activity. The magical healing powers of *Leahder* were what started me on the whole process of developing Wholistic Facial Care in the first place. *Leahder* dances with the skin cells, bringing a glow to

the face. I call *Leahder* "life for the skin."

In Wholistic Facial Care, *Leahder* is rubbed into the skin with a series of special strokes. These are described at the end of this chapter.

A special version of *Leahder* for use as needed on body skin exists as well.

2) *Smell, Sound and Colour.* Smell, sound and colour offer a healing language all their own to Wholistic Facial Care. Smell, sound, and colour carry messages which deeply affect the awareness,emotions and mental state. These forms of energy are used to deeply relax clients and to relieve the effects of stress.

Smells, especially, are necessary to relieve stress at the emotional and mental levels. Relaxing the mind and emotions is an important part of Wholistic Facial Care, since so much illness begins with repressed emotions and negative thoughts. Smells evoke emotion and sensation, and also have psychological effects. Smells also enhance the experience of taste, colour, sound and memory. Many people I have treated compare the smells to something. The same smell will have a different association for each person. Often different people will also find the same smell pleasant or unpleasant.

In Wholistic Facial Care the practitioner offers smells as therapy by putting essential oils on a facecloth which has been dipped in hot water and then draped over the client's face. In contact with heat, the essential oils quickly transform into vapour, and it is this vapour which relaxes stressed emotional and mental states. Smelling these vapours simply makes people feel good. In fact, smells can transport people into states of euphoria, just as music and colour can. In general, smell therapy can be very constructive, helping to build up a positive attitude to life.

The use of *Leahder* and smells in combination creates ideal conditions for facial rejuvenation.

Music in the background during the treatment further enhances mental and emotional relaxation. Music powerfully affects consciousness and reaches all levels of the emotions. It changes clients' moods and state of awareness. Some musics create excitement, energy and even aggressive feelings, while others encourage sensitivity and caring. Music can clear the psyche of anger, fear, worry and sorrow.

By selecting the music for the treatment environment with care, the practitioner helps clients relax and invigorate themselves.

Like smell and music, colour profoundly affects the psyche and feelings and complements and enhances the treatment process. Coloured gels over light bulbs create different colours; a dimmer switch for each bulb controls the intensity of the colour.

The practitioner chooses the colour or combination of colours used during a treatment based on his or her sense of an individual's needs at the time. For instance, a combination of green and white light relaxes the whole system, while red light warms and energizes. Each of the colours has its own effect.

3) *Food Therapy.* As a Wholistic Facial Care client you will be encouraged to fast regularly to rejuvenate the system,

to follow an internal cleansing diet at regular intervals and to switch to a lighter, healthier diet in general. The vast majority of people find it highly beneficial to eat less meat and refined sugars and more whole grains, vegetables, beans, nuts, seeds and fruits. As well, your practitioner may suggest freshly squeezed juices as tonics for the system or as a possible remedy for a specific problem.

The quality of our food and drink affects the quality of our blood. When our blood quality improves, a chain reaction of positive changes throughout our whole system begins.

You will find extensive information about health supportive eating and drinking in Chapters 5 and 6.

Organization of Treatment

At your first appointment with a Wholistic Facial Care practitioner, he or she will ask you to complete a questionnaire. The answers you give will assist the practitioner in designing a program that meets your special needs. It will include a cleansing program, general advice on diet, and treatment to damaged skin. The practitioner will also have been trained to stay alert to changes in your condition as the treatment progresses.These may require that adjustments be made to your individual program.

The practitioner may also feel that outside resources would help you. Keeping in mind a wholistic perspective that includes conventional scientific knowledge as well, he or she may suggest other therapies that would be beneficial to you. I personally often enrich treatments with reflexology, as it increases the effectiveness of my other work. Your practitioner may also suggest books to expand your knowledge of natural healing, in areas appropriate to your needs.

Most people need weekly Wholistic Facial Care treatments at the beginning of the treatment program. Regular treatments work most effectively, scheduled for the same time of the same day each week. At some point it will become clear that you need a treatment only every two weeks and finally only once every two or three months for maintenance.

How long the whole process takes depends on your health history, the nature of your current skin problems and your personal make-up. Each one of us has a unique rhythm of healing. Alternative therapies which respect your individuality cannot offer instant cures. Each treatment, however, will increase your strength and balance, and prevent further development of the cause of the problem. It is important to allow ourselves time for what we really need to become happy.

In general, a more intense schedule of treatments usually has to be followed somewhere from a few months to two years. The more you cooperate with your practitioner and your own healing process, the more quickly you will see results.

Facial Touch

I would like to end my part of this book (my clients have their say in the next chapter) with a gift to you. Following is a step by step description of the facial strokes

I use in my practice to apply *Leahder* to the face. You can give these to yourself or exchange healing touch with your friends. Not only your face but your entire body will feel wonderful afterwards.

Because of the deep sympathetic connection between the face and the body (See Chapter 4) a thorough facial touching sends energy to the internal organs, intensely relaxes your entire being and improves your overall functioning.

To receive the maximum possible benefit from the giving or receiving of facial touch, choose consciously to breathe deeply. You may also want to state to yourself, or out loud, that your intention with this action is to give and receive health and happiness. It can make quite a difference to the quality of the touch to have a focussed intention. Once you have stated your intention, open yourself in trust to the universe and healing energy, intuition and skill will enter your body.

The set of strokes that follows is first used to spread the *Leahder* dead cell remover over the face. When that has been done, wash the remover away with a hot face cloth and warm water. Then repeat the same series of strokes to spread *Leahder* food supply on the skin. Do not wash the food supply away. Your skin will quickly absorb it, without leaving behind any oily films.

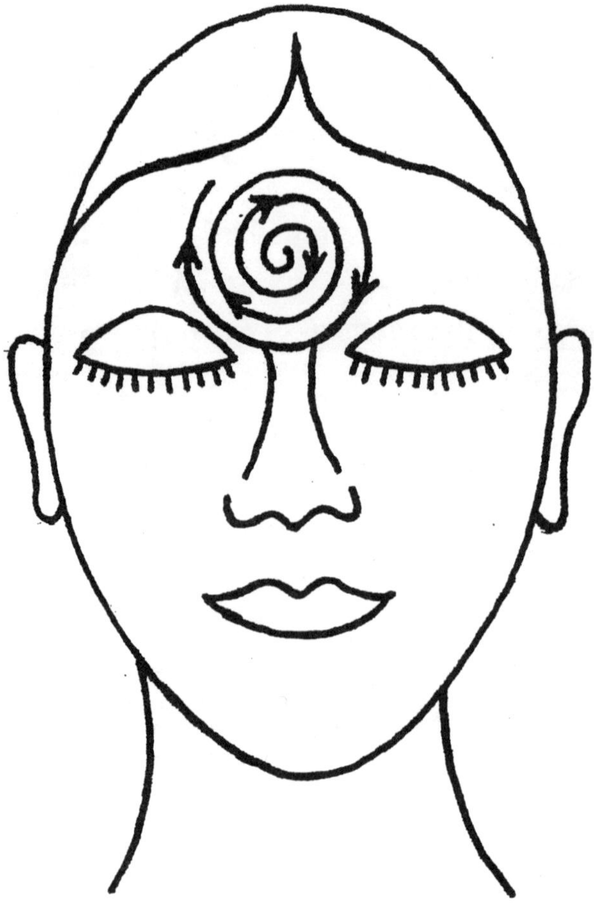

Figure 14.

Dip your fingers in the *Leahder* and place them in the centre of the forehead. Spiral outwards from the centre and loop back to the centre three or four times, using very light finger pressure. Finish with one finger in the middle of the forehead. Hold it there, pressing lightly, for a few seconds.

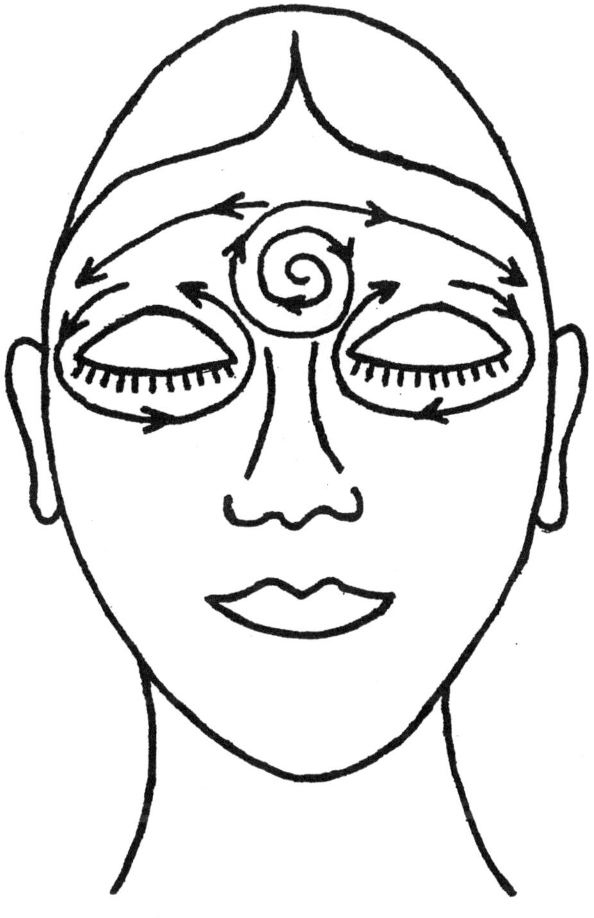

Figure 15.

Now make one more spiral, then slide the fingers of your two hands apart, towards the temples. From here circle the eyes three to four times. Work on wrinkles particularly, especially when you are removing the dead cells. If living cells are brought to the surface of the wrinkles, they can easily absorb the *Leahder* food supply. Over time the wrinkles will smooth considerably.

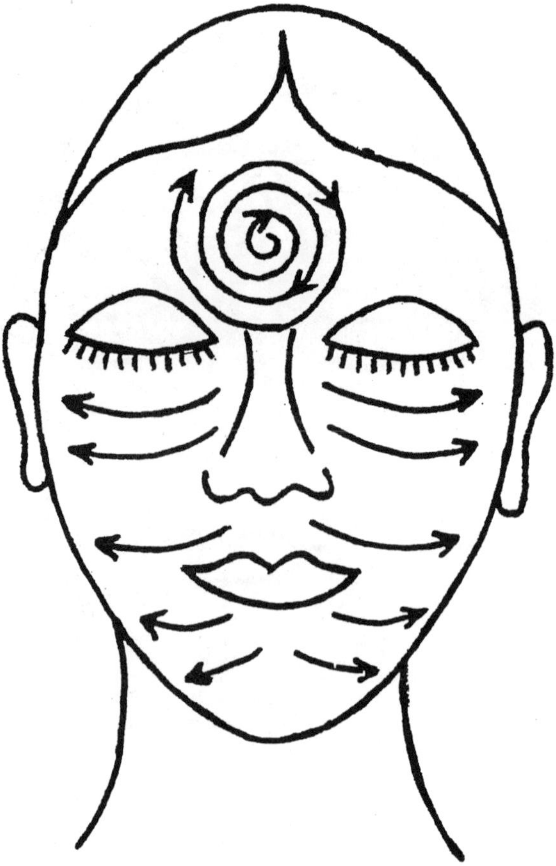

Figure 16.

If you are giving touch to someone else: Hold the palms for a moment over the forehead, cheeks and chin, lining up your hands (thumbs on the inside) on either side of the centre of the forehead. Then slowly draw the fingers out to the ears as if ironing the tension out of the face. Repeat the stroke to the ears three or four times.

Always use gentle strokes on the face and throat so your recipient(which might be you) feels the pleasure of being touched.

If you are giving yourself facial touch: The little fingers, rather than the thumbs of your lined up hands will be beside each other at the beginning of the stroke.

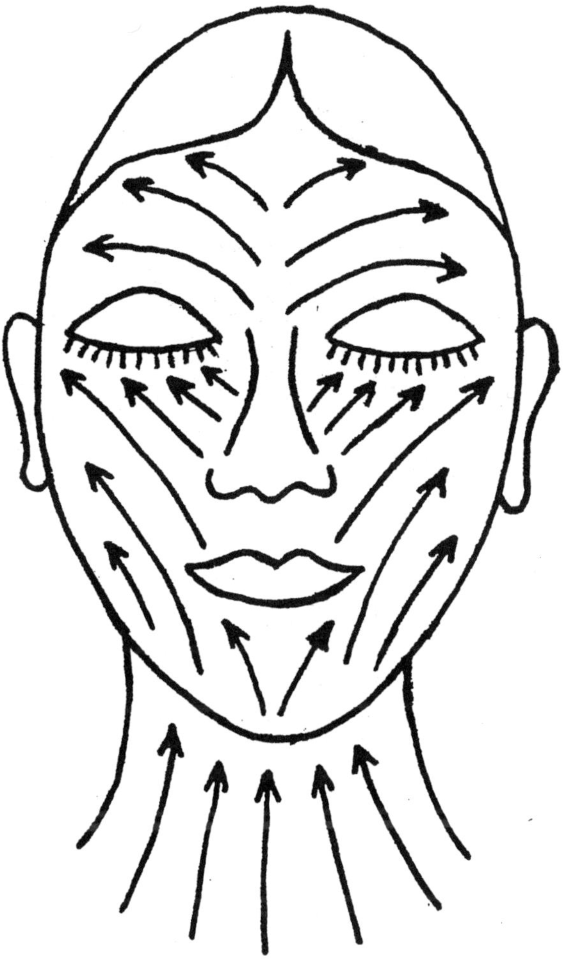

Figure 17.

Now stroke firmly upwards and lightly downwards a few times.

Move all the way from the throat to the hair line. On the throat use one hand after the other. During this stroke work particularly on wrinkles, behind and inside the ears, on the forehead and on the neck.

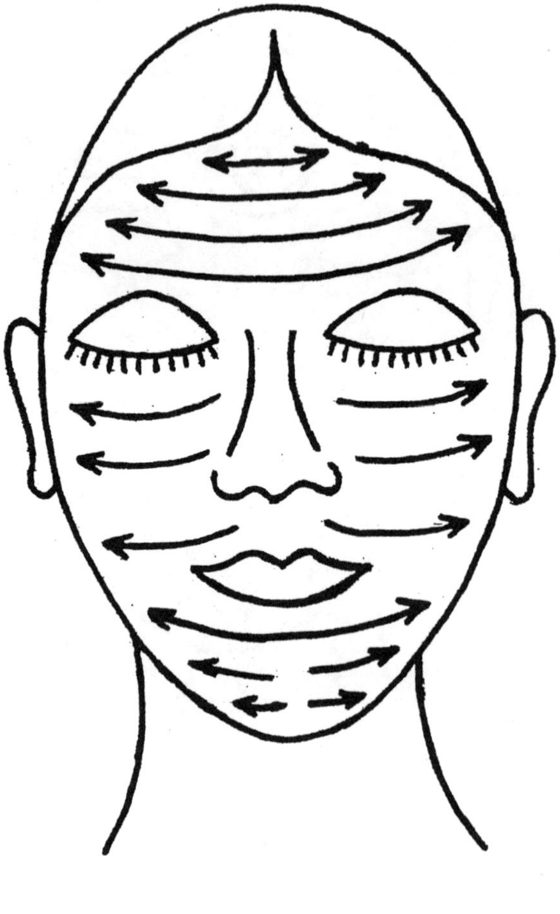

Figure 18.

Now put your palms over the face once more and again iron out all the tension from the face. Concentrate again on giving your recipient a chance to feel the pleasure of touch.

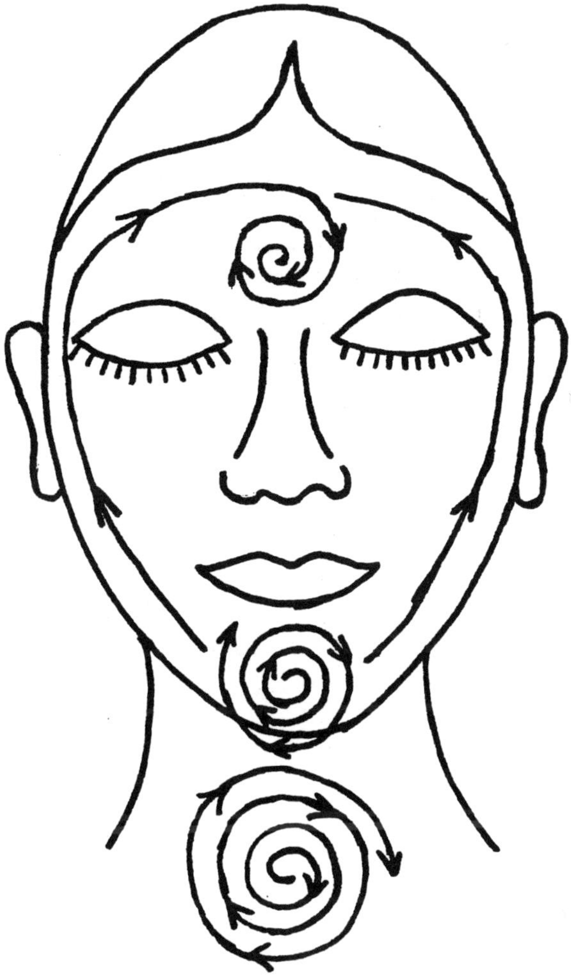

Figure 19.

Use these circular movements with a gentle touch to help the *Leahder* spread all over the skin.

Figure 20.

Finish in the same way you started, by working gently on the forehead chakra located between and slightly above the eyebrows. Finish with the finger at the centre, hold, press lightly for a moment and then slide the finger toward the crown chakra located on top of the head. Hold for a moment again and then slide the finger upward and out from the head.

Then place the palms over the whole face again for a few moments to give touch therapy, then gently take them away.

Chapter Eight

Testimonials

I have kept these testimonials anonymous to protect my clients. I offer them as an inspiration to you. The healing powers of nature really can restore our health and beauty, if we only open ourselves to the possibilities and faithfully work towards our goals.

One

I carried my skin problems, which I had thought I would outgrow as soon as I was out of my teen years, into adulthood. I had contact dermatitis and acne that on occasion was described as cystic, especially on the sides of my nose and chin (on the T-zone). The treatments with dermatologists were similar each time: antibiotics, astringents, lotions or creams and some advice on diet and stress relief. Not experiencing any break-out for a week or two was a source of happiness for me. I appreciated the doctors' help but I was feeling frustrated because of what seemed to be a vicious cycle which I felt was not doing my physical, emotional and mental systems any good.

I wanted something that would really clear out whatever was giving me all these skin problems and preferably treatment from someone who was using a natural approach (herbs, essential oils, etc.). I had read and heard of such treatments and was determined to find a program appropriate for my needs. Leah Dumbrava's ad appealed to me as it promised "beauty without creams" and "nutritional guidance."

From my first session with Leah, I was confident that I had met someone who could really help me. I felt an easy rapport with her and have since found my facial treatments very relaxing. Gradually I noticed fewer and fewer occurrences of skin eruptions and also an overall improvement in my facial skin tone and texture. My skin continues to improve and of late, some people who have known me for some time have remarked positively on it.

Leah also has encouraged me to look more closely at what my body needs and to what it responds best. For instance, I have become more conscious of what I eat and drink. An added bonus has been that it has become so much easier to maintain my weight.

Thanks to Leah, I not only got generous help with my skin and health problems but also for my emotional and mental well-being!

Two

Four years ago I developed acne on my face and back. This made me depressed and it seemed to affect my whole life in a completely negative way.

I began buying creams and I began to find that they were a total waste of time and money. I went to a specialist who gave me another cream which seemed to be burning my skin and this did not work either. I was absolutely miserable. Then I heard about Wholistic Facial Care. On Leah Dumbrava's advice, I tried a cleansing program of raw dandelion leaves juice (my drink during the day with honey) combined with fresh raw salads, lean meats and some cooked vegetables and one calcium and magnesium tablet per day. My skin began improving. It is almost completely clear and there is a healthy glow to my face. I feel really healthy and full of energy. I believe the change of diet and the dandelion juice with honey helped improve my health and well-being. My skin and health continue to improve and I feel really happy with myself. I would recommend Wholistic Facial Care to anyone with problem skin and to those seeking a higher level of health and energy.

Three

In the few months since I began following the Wholistic Facial Care program my energy has increased. I'm sleeping better. Since I was a child I have had very rough skin which has become beautifully smooth, thanks to the program. Now I am no longer ashamed of my appearance. I am 39 years old and have taken up yoga breathing and exercises again recently. I find I have more stamina than ever before. During the past year I have had lots of stress in my private life and my nerves were beginning to get a bit jagged. Now I am as calm and relaxed as I have ever been in my life. I no longer suffer from pre-menstrual tension. My psoriasis has disappeared and my whole health has improved a lot. The program has been like a magic potion to me.

Four

I have suffered from acne for most of my life. It was getting me down. I was told about the Wholistic Facial Care program. I was willing to try anything. In a few months I could see a big difference in my skin. I also lost weight quickly and safely without hunger and I have a lot more energy.

I would recommend the program to anyone with a skin problem.

Five

It is a great pleasure to recommend the service of Wholistic Facial Care. The philosophy of treatment struck a chord and I wanted to learn more. I have had an adult acne problem of many years, and so arranged for a facial. I noticed a marked improvement in my skin, improvement in texture, resilience, and balance, which lasted.

The *Leahder* preparation and some dietary changes led to further improvement. I was very impressed by the results. The program combined with aromatherapy made the underlying nervousness and agitation I had been feeling for months greatly diminish.

The reflexology sessions greatly enhanced the overall inner healing. I am thankful to Wholistic Facial Care, a natural healing method which brings us as clients so much benefit.

I highly recommend this inventive program with so many applications, a healing system that can be altered to fit individual concerns.

Six

In my case the Wholistic Facial Care program healed two persistent and extremely uncomfortable conditions - a rash and foot fungus. These had been active for three years and ten years respectively. Along with reflexology, nutritional supplements and dietary and lifestyle changes the conditions were healed in only four months. Then I continued with a preventative program.

It has been my good fortune to experience such a health program of this quality. I have never met anyone in the field of skin care with the expertise of this challenging wholistically minded care provider.

Seven

I read about Wholistic Facial Care in *Common Ground Magazine* and said to myself this will be the last time I try something for my complexion. I had tried everything available on the market, no matter what the cost.

The Wholistic Facial Care approach is working for me.

The activated ingredients continue working long after the treatment itself is over. My hair was also falling out in great quantities. After beginning the Wholistic Facial Care program, this problem has improved considerably. Now my hair is fuller and richer than it has ever been.

Eight

I want to say a few words about how grateful I am for what you've done for my skin. Until I heard about Wholistic Facial Care, I was using many kinds of cream with little result in the beginning. Later my skin became dull and lazy.

After only one wonderful treatment I noticed a difference in my complexion the next morning and looked forward to my next treatment. After a few months with Wholistic Facial Care I gained a fountain of youth in my skin. My face felt rejuvenated and the biological activity of the skin was reactivated. My skin looks healthier and brighter. Thank you for bringing a new glow to my face and new vitality to my body, which is noticed by everybody.

Wishing your new approach to facial care much success!

Nine

The Wholistic Facial Care program addresses not only the health of the skin but also the health of the body and the mind.

I was intrigued by Leah's "beauty without creams" approach to skin care and decided to give it a try. I am glad I did. Since the age of thirteen, I have suffered from acne which left my face scarred and pitted. As every acne sufferer knows, the scars were more than skin deep. They seeped into and deeply affected my self-image.

A long time dream of mine is to have beautiful, healthy, normal skin. After years of treatment with antibiotics, medicated cleansers and lotions, that dream was close to dying. Thanks to Leah, that dream is now close to becoming a reality.

The first treatment with Leah left me feeling relaxed, calm and very hopeful about the future. My face looked and felt so soft and smooth - it was incredible. After three months, there were no major break-outs and my skin was visibly changing - for the better. Now after nine months of Leah's care, guidance and encouragement, not only my skin but my health and self-image are on the mend.

I do definitely recommend Wholistic Facial Care.

Ten

I feel lucky to have met you and to have undergone your wonderful Wholistic Facial Care program. The results astounded me, as I had long ago given up on ever having healthy skin.

Due to contracting polio when I was only four years old, I grew up being unable to exercise or work out. As a result, my facial skin developed problems. It became greasy in some places, with very open pores, dry and itchy in others. No amount of cosmetic treatments, squeezing out of blackheads, or patting in of creams and astringents helped me. After I moved to Toronto, my skin became more and more tired and grey looking and my allergies worsened. I also developed a certain puffiness and lack of elasticity. I looked my age of thirty-eight.

The very first treatment with your natural ingredients made a dramatic difference. My skin "woke up" and started breathing. I could feel a youthful elasticity that remained for two weeks after the treatment. I felt and looked younger and people remarked on it a lot. Previously my skin had never been mentioned; it looked so drab and clogged. I was sold on continuing the treatments.

With a series of treatments you managed to clear my skin problems and reduce my skin's sensitivity to the elements. My face looks great and feels soft and resilient. Friends keep complimenting me on my healthy glow. I have no hesitations about recommending your system of healing. I wouldn't even have thought of my new modelling career if it weren't for my "new" skin.

I'm also pleased that you talked me into following an herbal internal cleansing program as it really enhanced the effect of your natural skin care ingredients and improved my general health. My chronic fatigue lifted, and symptoms of high toxicity throughout my body began to clear. The digestive tract cleansing and nourishing also made me feel more awake and energetic from dayone. I had not believed that would ever be possible. Previous fasting and cleansing I had done had taxed and tired my system. You offered me something that worked and I thank you for that.

You are a very knowledgeable person and I delight in talking with you. I like the fact that you practise what you teach and that your advice comes from your own personal experience. That makes it much easier to accept and to follow.

I am forever grateful.

Bibliography

Aihara, Herman. *Seven Macrobiotic Principles.* Oroville, California: The Georges Ohsawa Macrobiotic Foundation, 1977.

Aivanhov, O.M. *Love and Sexuality.* Frejus Cedex, France: Prosveta, 1989.

Baginski, Bodo J. and Shalila Sharamon. *Reiki: Universal Life Energy.* Mendocino, CA: Life Rhythm Publications, 1988.

Balch, James, M.D. *Prescription for Nutritional Healing.* Garden City Park, NY: Avery Publication Group, 1933.

Balch, Phyllis. *Prescription for Cooking.* United States: Pabbock Publications, 1937.

Ballentine, Rudolph. M.D. *Diet and Nutrition: A Holistic Approach.* Honesdol, PA: The Himalayan International Institute, 1978.

Barkas, Janet. *The Vegetable Passion: A History of the Vegetarian State of Mind.* New York: Charles Scribner and Sons, 1978.

Becker, Robert O., M.D. and Gary Selden. *The Body Electric: Electromagnetism and the Foundation of Life.* New York: William Morrow and Co., 1985.

Bieler, Henry, M.D. *Food is Your Best Medicine.* New York: Ballantine Books, 1982.

Burns, David D., M.D. *Feeling Good.* New York: William Morrow and Co., 1981.

Burns, David D., M.D. *The Feeling Good Handbook.* New York: William Morrow and Co., 1989.

Burroughs, Stanley. *Healing for the Age of Enlightenment.* New Castel, CA: Stanley Burroughs, 1976.

Cammon, Walter, M.D. *The Wisdom of the Body.* New York: W.W. Nortos & Co., 1939, 1963.

Carter, Mildred. *Body Reflexology.* New York: Parker Publishing Co., 1983.

Cerney, J.V. *Modern Magic of Natural Healing with Water Therapy.* West Nyack, NJ: Parker Publication Co., 1975.

Clark, Linda. *Get Well Naturally: Nature's Way to Health.* New York: The Devin-Adair Co., 1965.

Colbin, Annemarie. *The Book of Whole Meals*. New York: Ballantine Books, 1983.

Cecil, Lord Martin. *On Eagle's Wings*. New York: Two Continents Publishing Group, 1977.

Erasmus, Udo. *Fats and Oils*. Vancouver, Canada: Alive Book Publishing, 1986.

Esko, Wendy and Edward Esko. *Macrobiotic Cooking for Everyone*. United States: Japan Publications, 1980.

Klaper, Michael A., M.D., *The Cookbook for People Who Love Animals*. Umatilla, FL: Gentle World, 1981.

Lidell, Lucy, Giris Rabinovitch and Narayani Rabinovitch. *Yoga*. New York: Published by Simon & Schuster, 1983.

Mackie, Rona M. *Clinical Dermatology: An Illustrated Textbook*. Oxford: Oxford University Press, 1986.

McDougall, J.A., M.D. and M.A. McDougall. *The McDougall Plan*. Clinton, NJ: New Win Publishing, 1983.

Melvyn, Leonard, B.Sc., Ph.D. *The Dictionary of Vitamins*. New York: Thorson's Publishers, 1984.

Rona, Zoltan P., M.D., M.Sc., *The Joy of Health* . Willowdale, Ontario, Canada: Hounslow Press, 1991.

Schochet, Jacob Immanuel. *The Mystical Dimension*. Brooklyn, NY: Kemot Publishing, 1990.

Svoboda, Dr. Robert E. *Prakruti: Your Ayurvedic Constitution.* Albuquerque, NM: Geocom, 1989.

Tisserand, Robert. *Aromatherapy for Everyone.* London: Penguin Books, 1988.

Vogel, A. *Swiss Nature Doctor.* Teufen, Switzerland: A. Vogel, 1980.

Walker, Dr. N.W. *Back to the Land for Self Preservation.* Prescott, AZ: Narwalk Press, 1977.

————————. *Become Younger.* Prescott, AZ: Narwalk Press, 1949.

————————. *Colon Health.* Prescott, AZ: Narwalk Press, 1979.

————————. *Diet and Salad.* Prescott, AZ: Narwalk Press, 1940.

————————. *Water Can Undermine Your Health.* Prescott, AZ: Narwalk Pres s, 1974.

Index

Notes